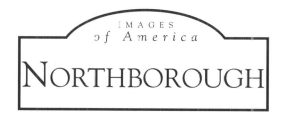

IMAGES
of America

NORTHBOROUGH

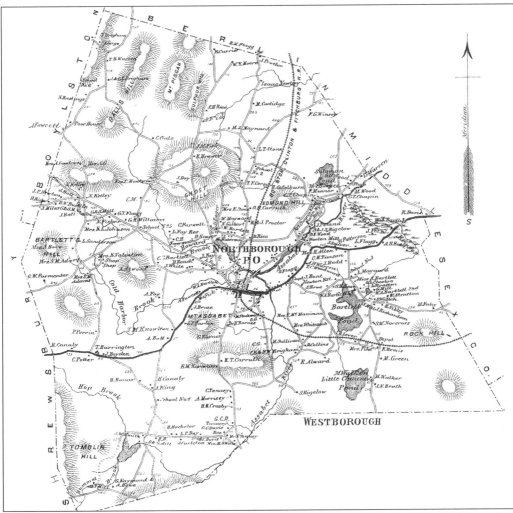

This 1870 map of Northborough depicts the town at the time when some of the earliest photographs in this book were taken. It is, in effect, a skeleton of modern Northborough, as the topography and the configuration of the major thoroughfares have changed little since then. As was common on 19th-century town maps, dwellings and their owners are indicated. It should be noted that street names have changed; also, the town adopted the present street numbering system only in the 1950s. The present-day addresses are used throughout this book.

Cover photograph: The students of Northborough High School, 1914–1915, included the following: Amory Gilbert, Clarence Walker, Gustav Carlson, Harlan Kimball, Harold Brigham, Preston Adams, Walter Carlson, Leslie Smith, Arthur Davidson, Ernest Williams, Sidney Walls, Frank Lilly, Clevis Stone, Clarence Potter, John Danckert, Hosmer Kimball, Rodney Leland, Charles Brigham, Dewey Balcom, Guerdon Bennett, Francis Gilbert, Edward Maynard, Daisy Balcom, Mildred Felt, Ruth LaPorte, Esther Bigelow, Cora Bigelow, Louise Eldridge, Marion Wheeler, Gertrude Picard, Dorothy Corey, Faith Duplessis, Marion Parmenter, Mary Eldridge, Mabel Van Ornum, Helen Gates, Ruth Russell, Myrtle Johnson, Grace Lawrence, Myrtle Lewis, Hulda Anderson, Elizabeth Hilliard, Madeline Brown, Ruby Lilly, Sarah Nelson, Irene Cobb, Florence Felt, and Theresa Danckert.

IMAGES
of America

NORTHBOROUGH

Northborough Historical Society

ARCADIA

First printed in 2000.

Published by Arcadia Publishing,
an imprint of Tempus Publishing, Inc.
2 Cumberland Street
Charleston, SC 29401

Printed in Great Britain.

Library of Congress Catalog Card Number: Applied for.

For all general information contact Arcadia Publishing at:
Telephone 843-853-2070
Fax 843-853-0044
E-Mail sales@arcadiapublishing.com

For customer service and orders:
Toll-Free 1-888-313-2665

Visit us on the internet at http://www.arcadiapublishing.com

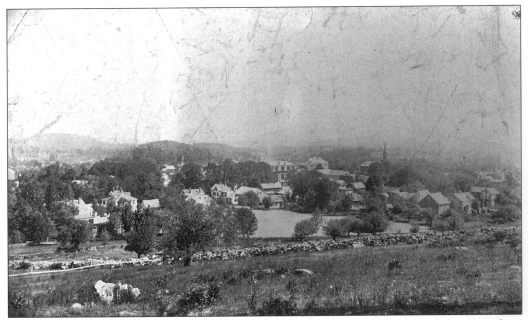

This late-1890s photograph shows the town center and northern stretches of the town from Assabet Hill, just south of the town center. The most prominent features are the church steeples. The St. Rose of Lima Church is on the left, and the Evangelical Congregational church (later the Trinity Church) is on the right. In the center is the town hall, with its mansard roof.

CONTENTS

ACKNOWLEDGMENTS

The compilers of this book, Ellen Racine and Robert P. Ellis, wish to thank the Northborough Historical Society Museum Trustees and Board of Directors for their support in this endeavor. Except where otherwise noted, the images in this book have been selected from the society's holdings.

We also wish to thank a number of people who have furthered the project by donating their time, knowledge, and expertise: Paul Derosier, Paul Desautels, Francis Doyle, Christine Ellis, Mike Ellsworth, David Hunt, Dorothy Hunt, Walter "Terry" Jones, Robert Kennerly, Gordon Maccabee, Ernest Racine, Betty Richardson, Janet Rogers, Mildred Sanders, Richard Sargent, Paul Shattuck, and Annette Warren.

Northborough Historical Society
Founded 1906

This hourglass is thought to have been the property of Mary Goodenow, who lived in what is now the eastern part of Northborough at the beginning of the 18th century (see page 12). Although it had been passed down through the family, the hourglass was eventually donated to the Northborough Historical Society. It is now on display in the society's museum, and has become the organization's official symbol.

INTRODUCTION

This book focuses on Northborough's second hundred years, the century between the 1860s and the 1960s. Although photographic images from late stages of the town's first century are necessarily rare, the reader will find in these pages some pictures of early buildings and some artists' renditions of early townspeople.

Even if photography had been invented before the late 1830s, the visual record would not have registered many important changes. In many respects, New England towns and villages in 1860 resembled ones that existed in 1660. The church remained the predominant institution. Houses continued to be framed in much the same way. People traveled on horseback and in wagons on unpaved roads. Commercial establishments did not differ greatly from residences, as they were often one and the same. Materials and styles of clothing varied little. Overall, people's *thought* may have changed between 1650 and 1850, but those thoughts did not greatly affect outward appearances.

In a curious way, the same generalization holds for the last few decades of the 20th century. Throughout this period, the automobile dominated land travel and the modern aerodynamic styling of automobiles was well established by the 1960s. Town centers had already become largely commercial, and the trend away from centralization had begun. This trend was spurred by a network of interstate highways—one of which sliced through northern Northborough in 1968—and other high-speed thoroughfares. Trees had already thinned as electrical poles and wires multiplied along downtown streets. Houses changed somewhat in style, but newer architecture usually imitated or combined long-established designs.

Our lives have changed profoundly in the past few decades, but these changes involve things that do not show, especially outside the home or workplace. Electronic innovations, especially the personal computer and the internet, alter our view of the world. However, we do not look *at* them so much as look *through* them. The development of the birth control pill in the 1950s (in which a Northborough resident played a key role) has profoundly affected social life, but not in ways that the eye of a camera normally catches. If a latter-day Rip Van Winkle were to walk into town, having been asleep since 1965, he would simply see more of the things he was used to seeing.

The map on page 2 depicts Northborough in 1870. The new town hall stands just left of the railroad tracks where they cross the town's rather serpentine Main Street, indicated by a heavy line below the Northborough Post Office. The photograph on page 9 shows the town hall under construction. Its humble predecessor had been about 200 yards south of Main Street at the edge of the First Church Common. In the memory of many residents alive in 1870, that church had been the *only* church. Before the new town hall was erected, the civic and religious life of town had centered on that church green.

A modest business section—a pharmacy, a few artisans' shops, and a general store containing a post office—had existed earlier on Main Street, but now the village was ready for a downtown. After an 1871 fire destroyed, among other structures, the buildings on both corners of Main and South Streets across the street from the town hall, many larger commercial buildings were erected. The railroad had come to town a few years earlier, in 1853, connecting merchants with markets and residents with friends and relatives. On the banks of local streams, sawmills and gristmills gave way to larger cotton and woolen factories. These factories were not large by the standards of Lowell or Lawrence, but they employed several hundred workers. In various shops around town, entrepreneurs were manufacturing products, such as combs, buttons, piano keys, and for a few years near the end of the century, some of the most modern cameras yet devised. By 1897, it was not necessary to hitch up or saddle up to visit neighboring towns; one could ride south to Westborough, east to Marlborough, and west to Worcester by electric car.

When Dr. Joseph Allen, once the town's only minister and most influential educational authority, died in 1873, one Catholic and three Protestant congregations were flourishing. The new high school building near the Unitarian church had been open since 1860. While younger children that year still walked to district schools as they had since the school's establishment, most students by 1895 were conveyed in "barges" to a centrally located school. Photographers were now peering into classrooms, and students routinely gathered for class pictures.

Two pairs of events, each of which occurred in close succession, exemplify the new importance of the visual record. In 1866, Northborough celebrated its centennial, even while it pondered a suitable tribute to veterans, living and deceased, of the recently concluded war. In 1919, Northborough sought to honor its World War veterans just three years after observing the town's 150th anniversary. We learn of the town's observances of the 1860s chiefly through the printed word; for those of the second decade of the 20th century, however, images abound. By comparison, the photographic record of the 1966 bicentennial, though technically more advanced, is no more ample than that of 50 years earlier.

The changes of the first six decades of the 20th century are too numerous to mention here, and even this book cannot properly do them justice. The 218 images in this book, however, do provide a representative sampling of the places where people resided, worked, worshiped, studied, and shopped while giving us glimpses of their social and recreational lives. These images bring home to us some familiar sights in earlier guises and other once-familiar sights that exist now only in recollection—reinforced and sharpened by the enduring photographic record.

One

LANDMARKS

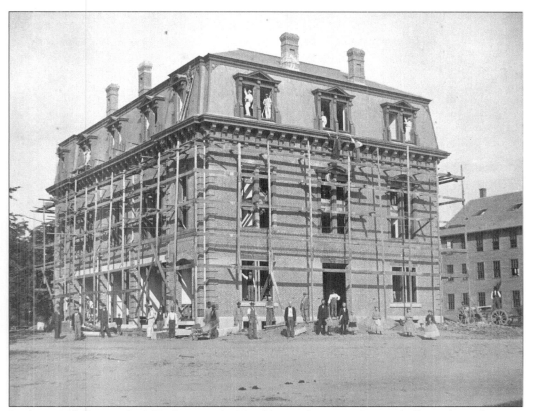

In this carefully posed 1867 photograph, Northborough's second town hall is taking shape in the town center. The bricks have come from Alonzo Howe's brickyard, 2 miles away. The mansard roof is a currently popular architectural feature. Workers and a number of townspeople have managed to become part of the scene, many of them possibly facing a camera for the first time in their lives.

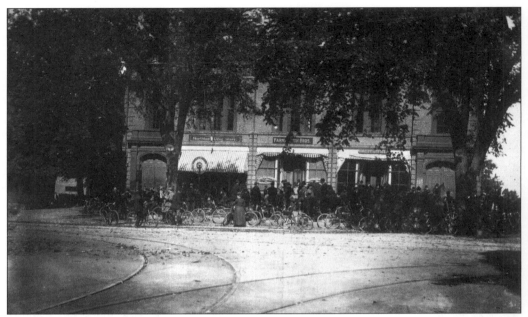

In 1899, bicycles are becoming the rage. On October 1, this group of wheelmen assembles at the town hall on Main Street. The first floor of the building houses Claude T. Shattuck's drugstore, Farnsworth Brothers general store, and the post office. In the foreground, trolley tracks, which had been laid only two years earlier, run east and west, branching off south toward Westborough.

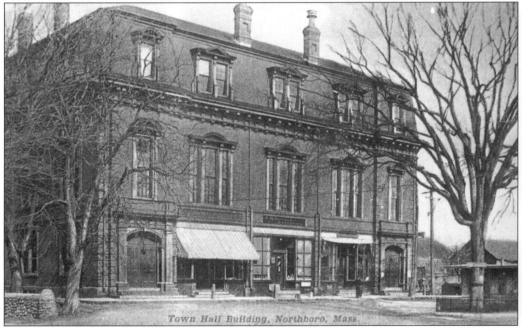

An air of repose hangs over the town hall in this c. World War I postcard. Not too much has changed. The middle store is now operated by E.P. Daniels. One of the trees in front has vanished. The small building at the right is the railroad station.

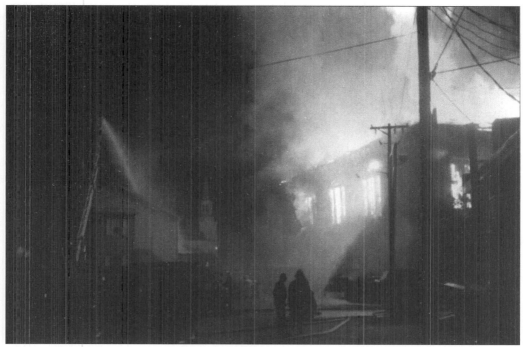

It is now early morning, September 18, 1985, and tragedy has struck. The town hall is being consumed by a fire of mysterious origin. A firefighter and his companion view the rear of what is left of the building that was the center of town activity for decades. The ghostly spire of Trinity Church, two blocks to the east, is visible just to the left of center.

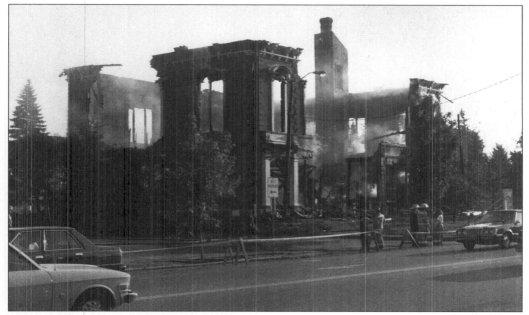

A few hours later, motorists cruise past the smoking remains of the town hall. The Shattuck Pharmacy, having moved across the street some years earlier, is safe; the town government has shifted to the former high school building one-quarter mile to the east. The destroyed building recently was being renovated by a developer who planned to build a replica on the site.

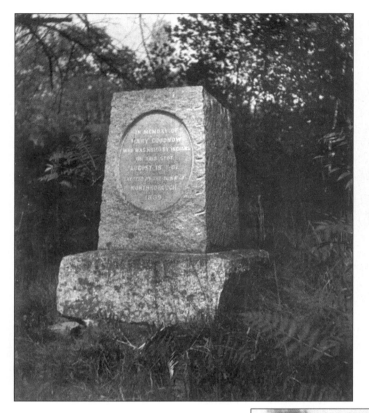

On August 18, 1707, Mary Goodenow, a young woman from one of only four families who settled on the tract that later became Northborough, suffered the consequences of a frontier conflict. Surprised by a local native tribe, she could not run fast enough to escape because she was lame. In 1889, the town erected this monument on the spot where she fell.

In 1907, the first full year of its operation, the Northborough Historical Society placed this stone just south of Main Street near the town's eastern border. The stone marks the spot where the garrison house of Samuel Goodenow withstood the Native American assault 200 years earlier. It was this refuge that daughter Mary Goodenow failed to reach.

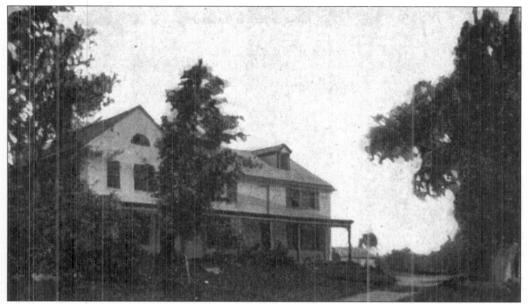

Until it burned in 1899, this building occupied the West Main Street site of the present St. Rose of Lima Church. Dr. Stephen Ball acquired it in 1765. His son Jonas Ball made it into a tavern featuring a commodious dining room and a ballroom. Stagecoaches on their way to Worcester stopped here for a change of horses. The establishment was later known as the Elm Tree Inn.

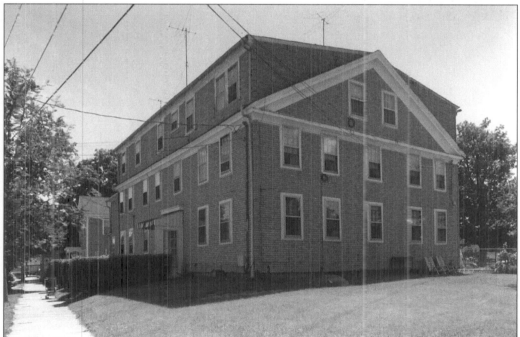

Another inn of Revolutionary times, this building—or at least part of it—constituted the Munroe Tavern. After the Civil War, Capt. Cyrus Gale purchased it and moved it northward on its block to its present location at 31 Blake Street in order to make way for the new town hall. Gale handsomely subsidized the town hall in return for a free hand in designing it.

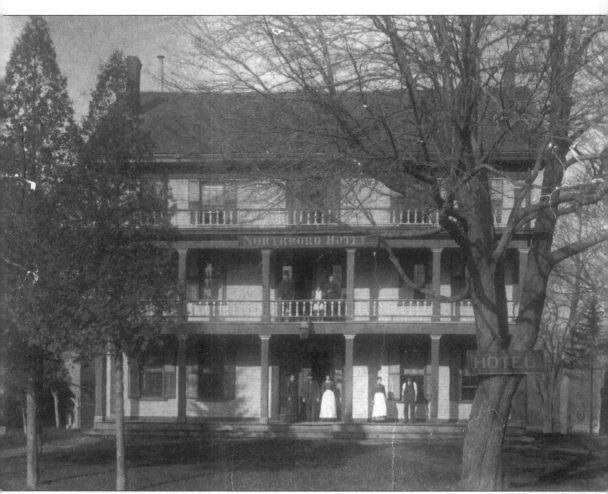

Shown is another hostelry of a town whose population never exceeded 2,000 people until the 20th century. The Northborough Hotel, dating from the Civil War era, faced Main Street just west of the Church Street intersection. The owners throughout its history were members of the Page family, but a long succession of managers operated it with varying degrees of success. In 1911, selectman Philip Hilliard staged a one-man raid on the hotel after learning that it was dispensing alcohol in an officially dry town. In later years, this comfortable-looking lodging house was called the Northborough Inn. When it was destroyed by fire in late 1926, its last operator decided to open a gasoline station there. This was surely a sign of the automobile age, as far fewer people had to stop in Northborough for overnight lodging than for a simple fill up. Not surprisingly, a filling station continues to occupy the site.

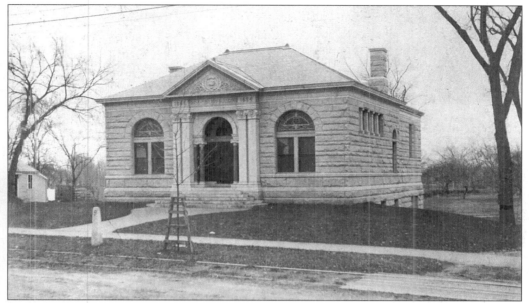

The Northborough Free Library, dedicated in 1895, is seen here as it appeared in the early 1900s. It replaced a pharmacy established by Dr. Stephen Ball II, whose house stands immediately east on Main Street (see page 33). The library was a gift of local philanthropist Cyrus Gale Jr., another neighbor (see page 42). It was expanded by an addition in 1975. Currently, another addition is planned.

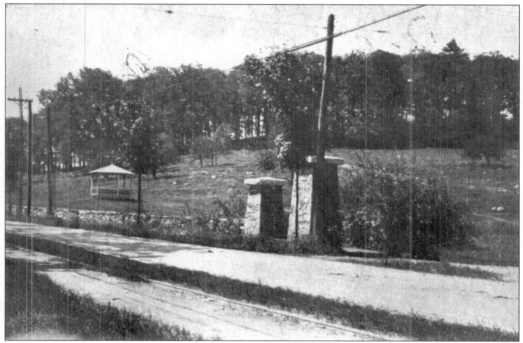

On the slope of Mount Assabet (once called Liquor Hill) is Assabet Park, another of Cyrus Gale Jr.'s gifts to the town. This tranquil oasis near the town center on South Street has long served Northborough residents. Seen here in the mid-20th century, the park has recently been reconfigured for preschool and elementary schoolchildren.

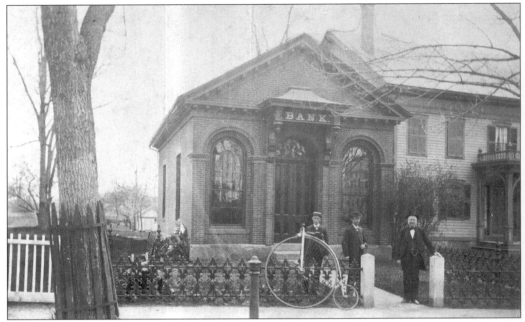

Three officials of the Northborough Bank pose in front of the building that housed the institution for almost a century after its establishment in 1854. It was the first bank in the immediate area and was an early member (1865) of the National Banking Association. Since 1950, the building has served as a post office, a newspaper circulation office, and the headquarters of any number of businesses.

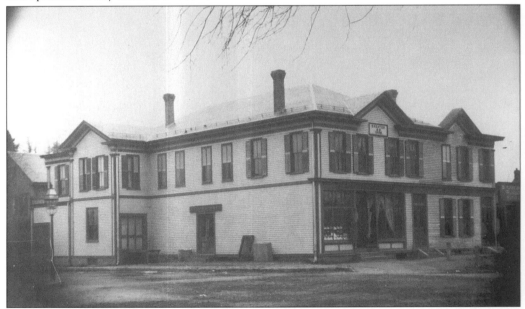

In 1871, Northborough's Great Fire destroyed several houses on both sides of South Street near Main Street, clearing the way for new commercial buildings. At the west corner of the intersection, Page's Block (later known as the Devine building) is pictured here not long after its construction in 1882. It accommodated a variety of business and professional enterprises until another fire consumed it in 1979.

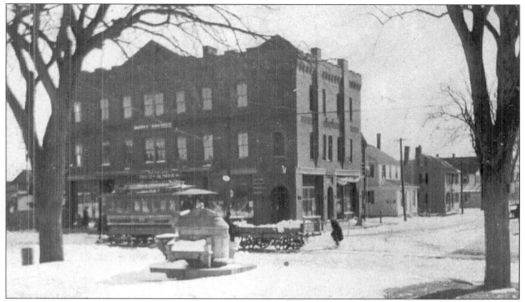

The three-story Winn-Whitaker building was erected in 1882 on the southeast corner of Main and South Streets. In this c. 1910 view from the town hall across the street, another hotel, the Assabet, occupies the building's upper floors. This establishment garnered even more official disapproval than the Northborough Hotel, not only for liquor violations but also for harboring prizefighters as residents. This building was trimmed to two stories in the early 1960s.

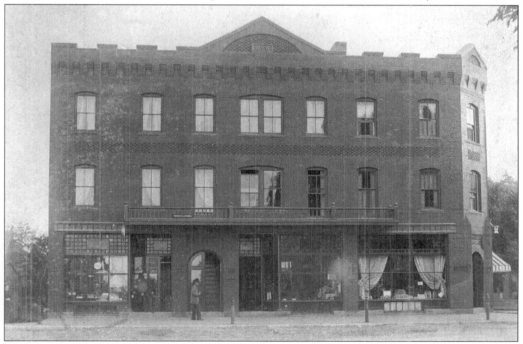

The sign to the right of the open stairway of the Winn-Whitaker building reads "Dr. Oakes," confirming that this photograph was taken between 1887 and 1890. Several signs in the window of Seth Emery's corner pharmacy entice us with "ice cold soda." The numerous hitching posts along the street indicate the patrons' common mode of travel.

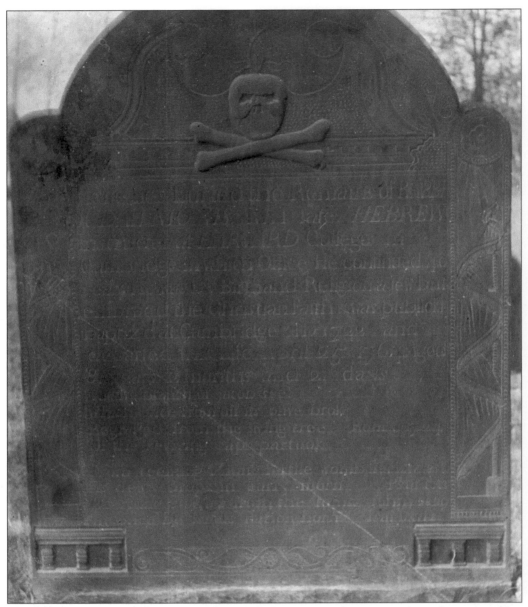

This curious gravestone has long attracted the attention of townspeople and tourists alike. Judah Monis was most likely born in Italy. He attended Jewish academies in Leghorn and Amsterdam and was consecrated a rabbi. Coming to America in 1720 at the age of 37, he settled in Boston. Two years later, he converted to Christianity and accepted an appointment to teach Hebrew at Harvard. He was a recognized scholar at a time when Harvard could boast few such people. He compiled the first Hebrew grammar text published in America. He and one of his students, John Martyn, married sisters from Cambridge: Abigail and Mary Marrett, respectively. In 1745, Martyn was appointed the first minister of the new north precinct meetinghouse of Westborough (the future First Church of Northborough). After Monis's wife died in 1761, the former rabbi retired after 40 years at Harvard and came to live with his Martyn in-laws. He died in 1764 at the age of 81 and was buried in the cemetery behind the meetinghouse.

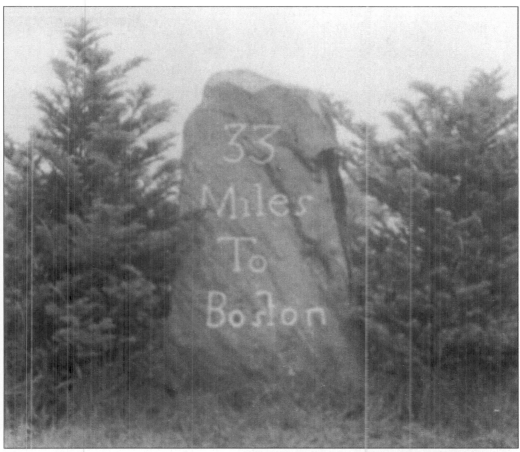

This rough-hewn milestone stands on Northborough's East Main Street, which was a section of the Boston Post Road until the early 1930s, when a new stretch of highway to the south supplanted it. Several such milestones survive along the Boston Post Road, but this is the only one remaining in Northborough.

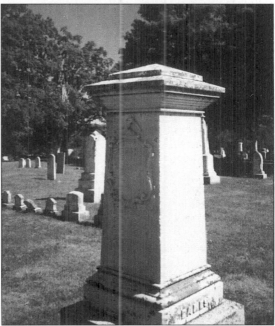

Members of the Eames family rest in the Howard Street Cemetery. Civil War volunteer Warren Eames wrote to his father on September 9, 1861, "All the regiments here are quite discontented because they are not sent across the Potomac River. I hope they will either kill or cure us by trying the experiment." He got his wish. A few weeks later, he fell in the Battle of Ball's Bluff.

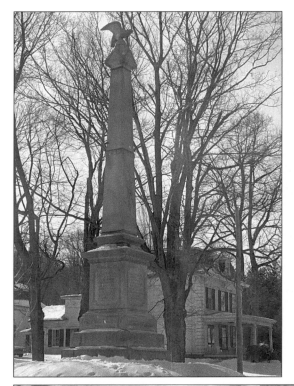

This column at West Main and Monroe Streets bears the names of the 29 Northborough men who died in the Civil War. Columbus Eames, whose son Warren Eames became the first Northborough casualty of the war, chaired the committee in charge of the memorial, which he designed himself. The memorial was dedicated on September 17, 1870—the eighth anniversary of the Battle of Antietam, in which five Northborough men perished.

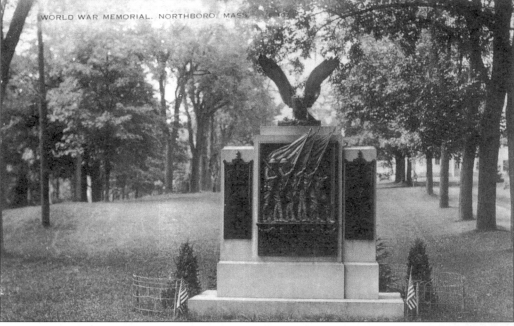

Of Northborough's memorials to its soldiers, the World War I monument on the grounds of the First Church is the most aesthetically distinguished. The bronze relief of infantrymen appears to have been strongly influenced by Augustus Saint-Gaudens's famous design for his memorial to Robert Shaw's black Civil War regiment, which stands on Beacon Street across from the State House in Boston.

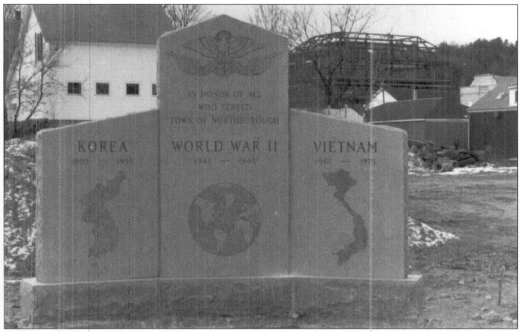

For many years Northborough had no suitable memorial to the townspeople who served in World War II. Finally, veterans' agent Richard Perron designed this tripartite monument commemorating veterans of that war in addition to those who served in the Korean and the Vietnamese conflicts. Erected at the corner of Pierce and Hudson Streets, the monument was dedicated on Memorial Day of 1988. The replica of the burnt-out town hall rises in the background.

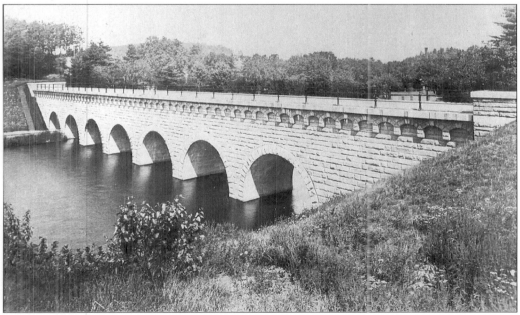

No longer in use since it began to leak water onto Hudson Street beneath it, the Metropolitan District Commission's aqueduct bridge over the Assabet River remains a distinctive Northborough landmark. For views of its construction in the 1890s, see pages 86 and 87.

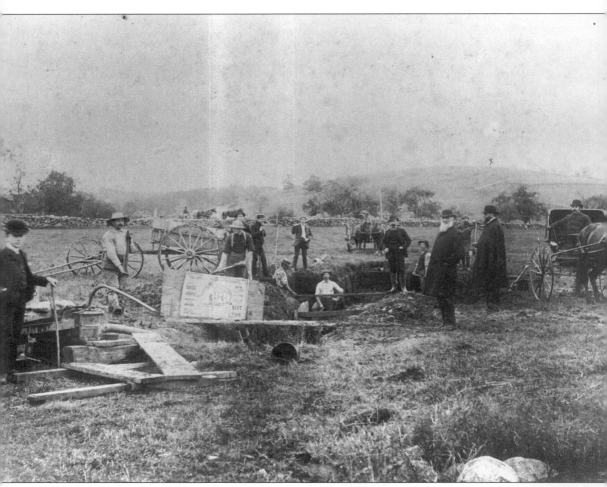

On November 17, 1884, workmen digging a trench on William Maynard's farm on West Main Street near the Shrewsbury line discovered fragmentary bones and teeth of a large animal. The same day, Maynard took samples to a Shrewsbury doctor, who in turn showed them to a group of naturalists and antiquarians in Worcester. These men visited the site the next day, but because of the recent hoax of the "Cardiff Giant," they tended to remain skeptical of the find. Three days later Alexander Agassiz, the curator of the Museum of Comparative Zoology at Harvard University, judged the teeth to be those of a mastodon. The mastodon was an elephant-like creature living perhaps 10,000 years ago. It was a probably hairy animal with tusks as long as 8 or 10 feet. Most of the mastodon's remains are in the Worcester EcoTarium, but a few fragments are on display in the Northborough Historical Society Museum.

Two

PEOPLE AND THEIR HOMES

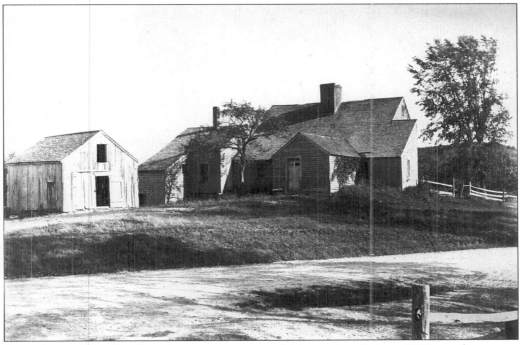

Luther Rice (1783–1836) was born in this house, which stood until about 1900 on what is now Lincoln Street. A tireless missionary and promoter of religious education, Rice earned a reputation as an important leader of the Baptist Church. He established the first national Baptist periodical and founded Columbian College in Washington D.C., which evolved into today's George Washington University. Another house memorializing him now occupies the site.

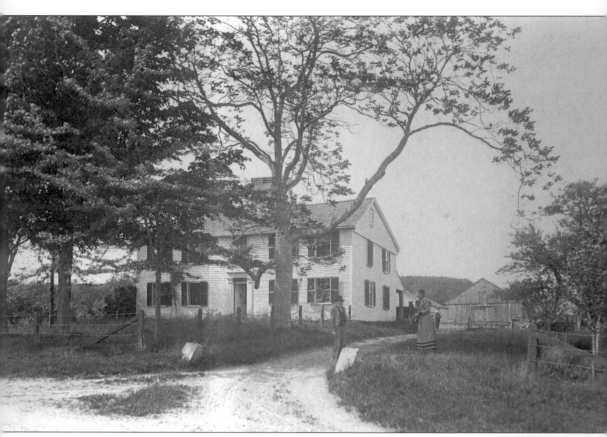

This is how the Holloway house at 302 Church Street looked in 1894. In 1744, Col. William Holloway was one of about 40 heads of families in what is now Northborough. Because some of these families had to walk as far as 5 miles to church, they successfully petitioned the town of Westborough for the status of separate precinct, thus entitling them to their own meetinghouse. The organizational meeting of the new North Precinct of Westborough took place on November 15, 1744, at the Holloway house. The meetinghouse rose the following year and in 1766, the Town of Northborough was incorporated. Dating from 1711, this is perhaps the oldest extant house in town. It may have been used as a garrison during the French and Indian War. Throughout most of the 19th century, the house belonged to the Williams family. Pictured are George Williams and his daughter Ellen Williams.

Ellen Williams, the last of her family to occupy the Holloway house, earned a reputation as an independent and intellectual woman. In her earlier years, she taught persons with developmental disabilities, in Syracuse, New York. For the last three decades of her life, she served on the board of library trustees in Northborough. She died in 1917 at the age of 78.

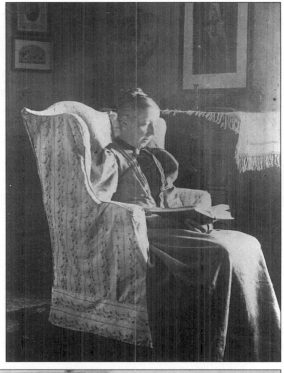

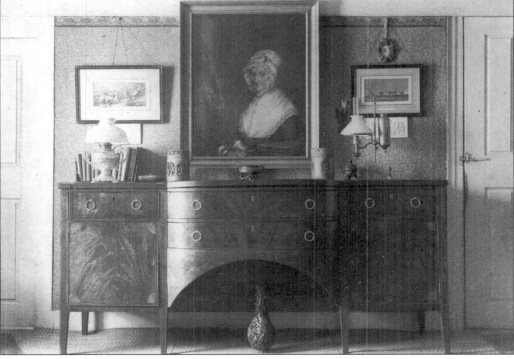

These were some of the furnishings of the Holloway house during the time of the Williams family. George Williams died in 1895, and three years later his daughter sold the house. Subsequent owners have done considerable restoration work on it.

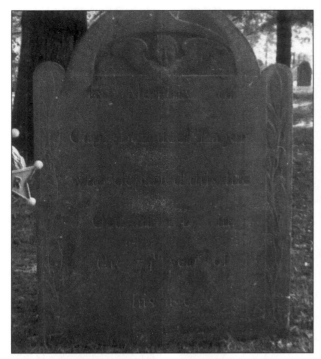

For nearly two centuries, a stone near Davis Street marked, *not* the grave of Bezaleel Eager, but rather the spot where the 73-year-old veteran of two wars was thrown from his horse and fatally injured on October 31, 1787. Vandals destroyed the stone with its inscription, but this stone in the cemetery on Howard Street marks his actual grave.

The older part of the Bezaleel Eager house at 455 West Main Street may date from 1711, rivaling the Holloway House in antiquity. Eager served as a lieutenant in the French and Indian War. In the Revolutionary War, he served as a captain, probably on the staff of Gen. Artemas Ward of nearby Shrewsbury. He was also active in local and state politics.

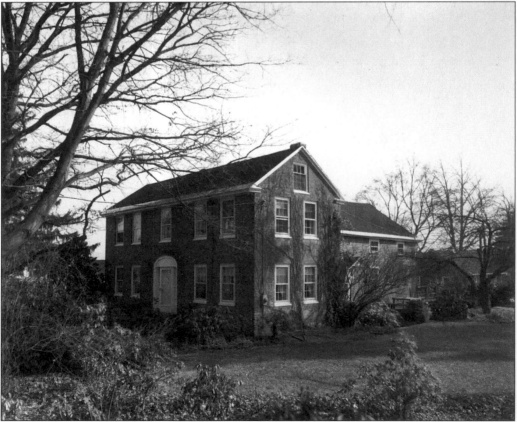

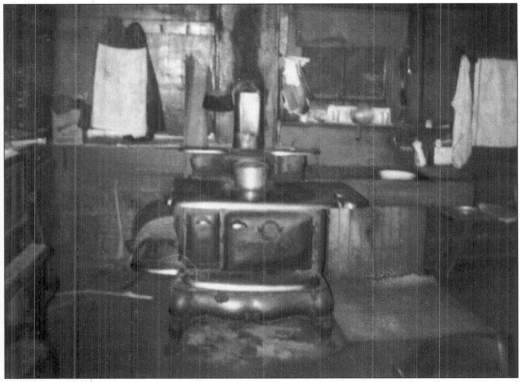

Edith DeArmond kept house in her 18th-century Maple Street cottage until 1952. It may surprise younger readers that she and no doubt others with roots in the 19th century continued to use kitchen furnishings such as these as late as the 1960s.

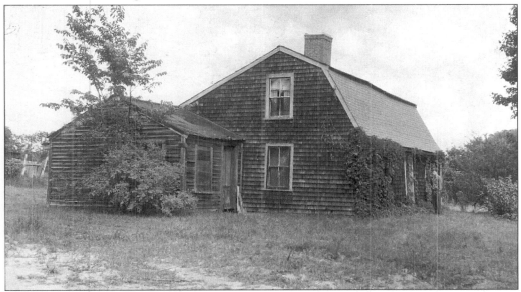

Members of the Newton family once lived in this house. Deacon Paul Newton and Paul Newton Jr. marched with the Northborough minutemen in the Revolutionary War. Late in the 19th century, the property became the DeArmond family farm. The town acquired this property in order to build the Marguerite Peaslee School.

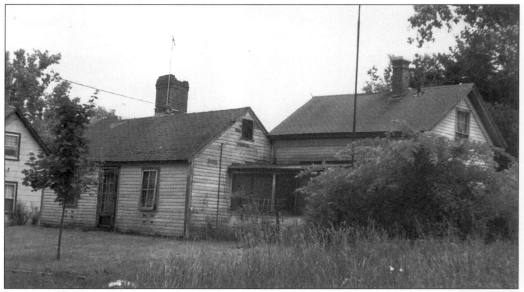

Like the DeArmond house, this house at 32 East Main Street persisted from the 18th century into the 1960s. The house was demolished after its last owner, Stanley E. Sullivan, died in 1968. Another dwelling now stands on the site.

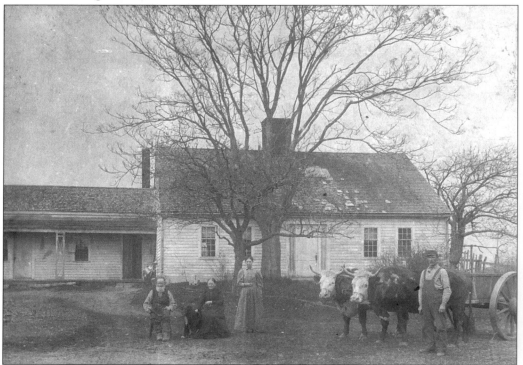

The bearded Warren Moore and his wife pose stiffly outside their farmhouse in 1897 with a woman who is perhaps their daughter, their dog, two oxen, and a hired hand. This property belonged to members of the Maynard family in the late 18th and early 19th centuries. It was long the only house on what would be known as Moore Lane. By the mid-20th century, the house had fallen into ruin.

Rev. Peter Whitney was the second town minister; he served from 1767 to 1816. In 1793, Whitney published a history of Worcester County, making him Northborough's first town historian. A copy of his book, dedicated to John Adams and printed by Isaiah Thomas in Worcester, was an early part of the Northborough Library collection. It is now in the Northborough Historical Society collection.

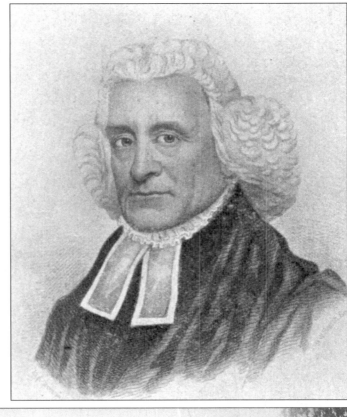

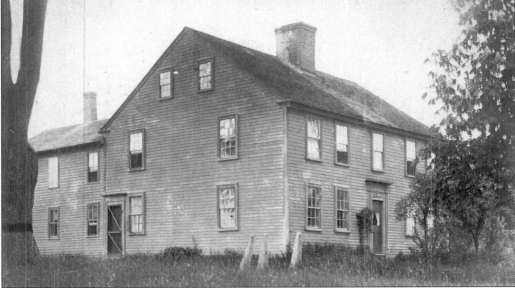

While preaching a sermon on April 26, 1780, Rev. Peter Whitney was handed a note informing him that his house was on fire. After glancing at the note, he continued the sermon, returning home only after the service to find the parsonage a total loss. The present owners of the rebuilt parsonage at 62 Whitney Street have restored much of the late-18th-century interior to its original condition.

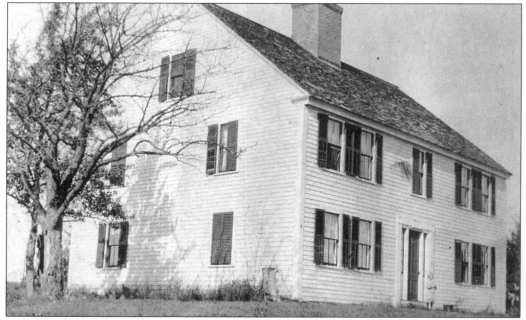

Arriving in Northborough *c.* 1727, Jonathan Livermore built this house at 500 Green Street in the northwest corner of the town. Although he was spry enough on his 100th birthday in 1800 to ride his horse down Ball Hill to a military muster, he died the following year. His will withheld his grandson's legacy until the young man, who had gone to live in Canada, "quit the kingdom of Great Britain."

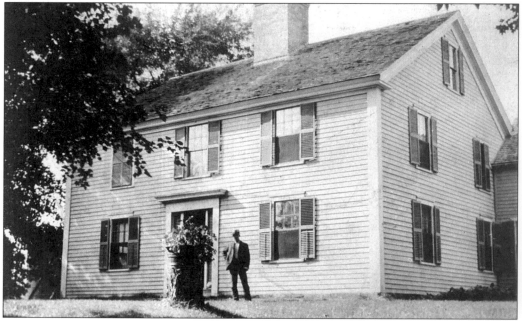

The surnames of the owners of this venerable property at 66 Green Street read like a historical Northborough *Who's Who:* Brigham, Hayward, Fay, Day, Buckley, Carlson, and Parkhurst. Because the Fays owned the property the longest, it is frequently called the Fay farm, even though there have been at least three other Fay farms in Northborough.

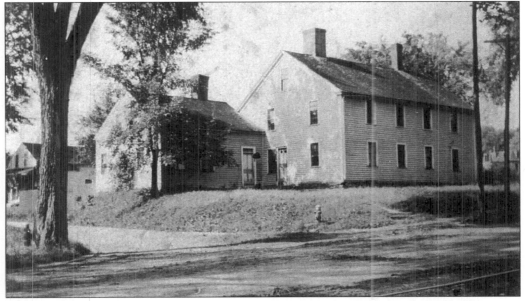

The Capt. Samuel Wood house rose in 1749 on Main Street just east of the Assabet River. Wood led his 50 Northborough minutemen to Boston on April 19, 1775. The house, now 97 Main Street, has known many owners since then, including Thomas H. Blair, a pioneer in the manufacture of cameras and film. Blair brought his business to town in 1894 but sold it to George Eastman five years later.

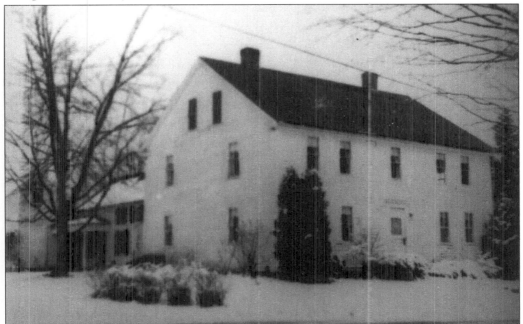

Thomas Billings built this house at Crawford and West Streets in 1734. At the time of the Revolutionary War, townsfolk judged him "inimically disposed towards this and the other United States of America." However, because he was old and crippled, Billings was punished merely by house arrest during the war. A religious outsider, he was considered Northborough's first Baptist many decades before the town had a Baptist congregation.

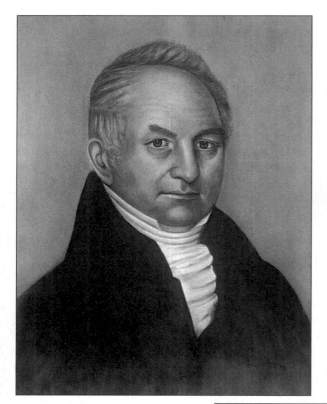

Dr. Stephen Ball II (1767–1850) ranks as one of the more colorful Northborough characters. He doubled as a pharmacist. One of his prescriptions was a salve called Unguentum Polychres. Among many other ingredients, it contained "green tobacco, cheese mallows, yellow pond lily root, Old David's Weed, and hog's lard." Ball also is credited with building the Smith Mill in the southwest part of town (see page 79).

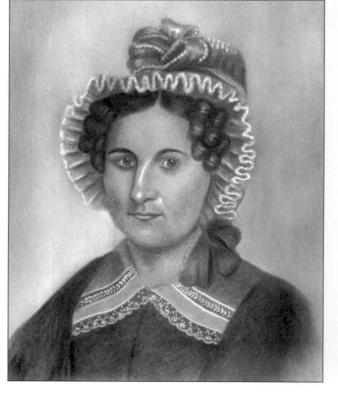

Dr. Stephen Ball married Lydia Lincoln, a member of an early Hingham family, several members of whom moved west to Northborough and Worcester. Like others of her family (see page 50), she possessed musical talent, and Ball bought her a Babcock piano, manufactured c. 1827. Delivered in an ox cart, the piano was the first such instrument ever seen in Northborough. It now rests in the Northborough Historical Society museum.

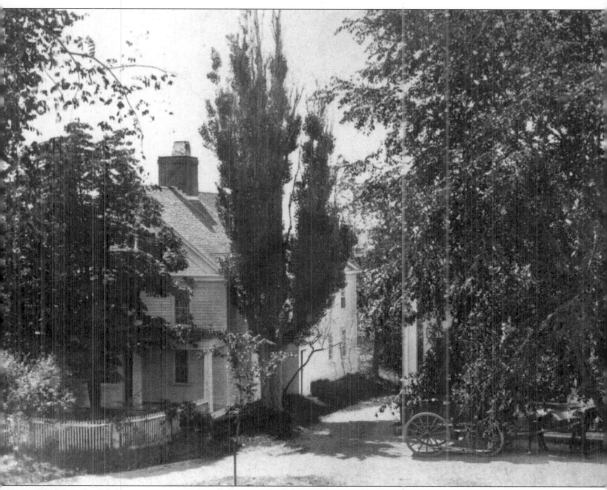

This early-20th-century postcard depicts a house that still stands at 38 Main Street. The distinctive picket fence found in the earliest photographs of the house—or at least a later re-creation of that fence—continues as a recognizable feature today. Built c. 1730 and acquired late in the same century by Dr. Stephen Ball II, the house remained in the family for more than 200 years, until Alice Manley Irwin died in 1993 at the age of 105. Its neighborhood, just east of the town center, has the largest concentration of older, little-modified houses in town.

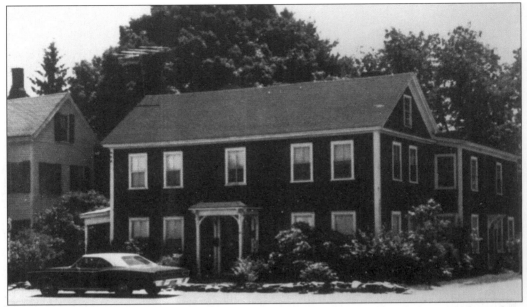

In 1832, when this red house on West Main Street facing Church Street belonged to blacksmith William Throop, the organizational meeting of the Evangelical Congregational church took place within. The house and Throop's blacksmith shop behind it stood until 1979, when they were replaced by the bank that is now on the site.

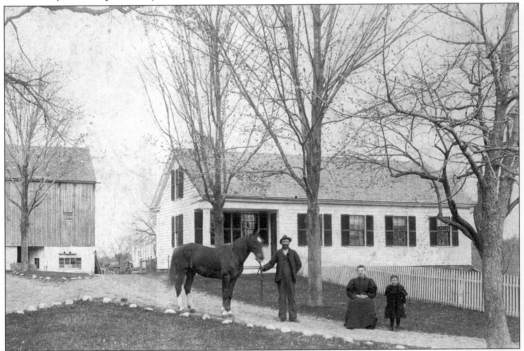

In 1740, Jothan Bartlett built a house on the site that eventually became 413 Main Street, using lumber from the Samuel Goodenow garrison across the road (see page 12). This house, which stood just west of the present Kingdom Hall of Jehovah's Witnesses, has been replaced by another. Norman Balcom and his family pose for this 1897 photograph.

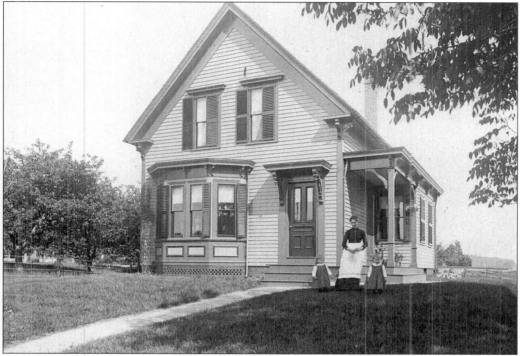

Florence Brigham Potter and her twin sons, Norman and Raymond, are seen at their 45 Summer Street home, c. 1889. Raymond Potter died young, but Norman Potter (who also appears in the brass band on page 113) became a bank director and town treasurer. Henry Corey bought this house in 1924, and his daughter Helen Corey lived there into her extreme old age. For pictures of Helen Corey, see pages 108 and 128.

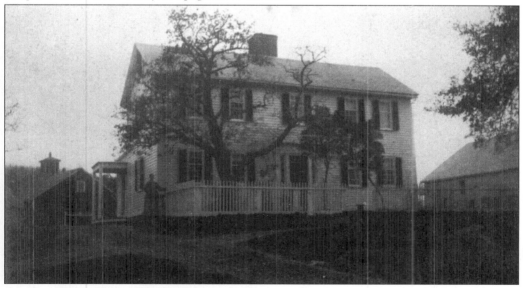

Another of Northborough's Fay farms is this house at One Mentzer Avenue. Built by Silas Fay in 1737, it was later sold to the Mentzer family. This farm once sprawled over hundreds of acres in the northwestern part of town. Well kept today, the house occupies a secluded spot north of Route I-290 on one of the streets truncated by the construction of the highway.

Elmer Valentine held forth in his boarding school for boys and girls from c. 1838 until his death in 1863. According to his granddaughter Edith, Valentine had a "sunny temper and humorous disposition" but also maintained a "commanding presence" that discouraged disobedience.

Rebecca Valentine was the daughter of Col. William Crawford. She and her husband bought the farm from Crawford and established a school there. She was credited with being a veritable mother to the two dozen or so children whc, at any given time, boarded there. This feat is made even more impressive by the fact that she had 15 children of her own.

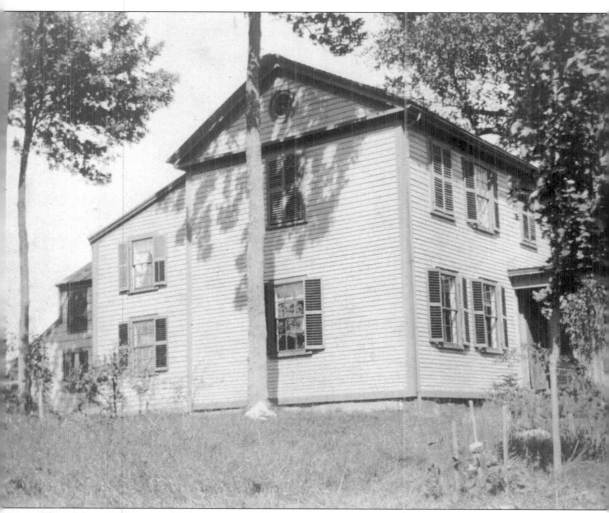

The Valentine house, which was originally much smaller, had to be enlarged to accommodate as many as 40 people. In the school across the road, Elmer Valentine placed great emphasis on penmanship, which to him was not just "making marks" but rather the art of writing both simply and beautifully. He told his students that "learning was no mere private pleasure of their own but a possession of actual use to the community." Among his students at an earlier school that he conducted in Boston were Charles Sumner, who later served as a U.S. senator, and Fanny Fern, who became an extraordinarily popular writer. Valentine's enthusiasm for teaching rubbed off on family members. His daughter Ellen maintained the school for a while after his death. His granddaughter Edith taught for 47 years and was responsible for providing much of the information known today about the Valentine Boarding School. Other Valentines have been teachers, even down to the present day.

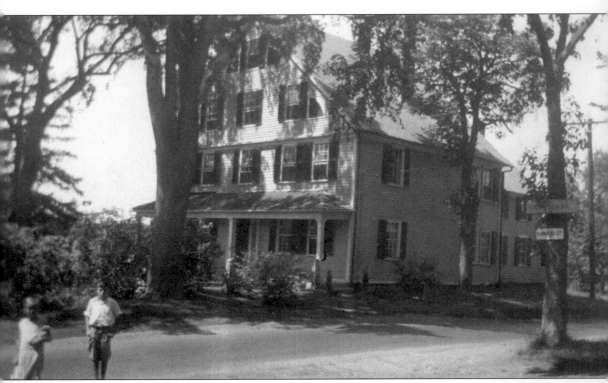

This house at 49 Church Street was built in 1818 for Northborough's new minister, Dr. Joseph Allen. Allen was the third and last of the men who could claim the title of town minister. He and his wife, Lucy Ware Allen, the daughter of Harvard College's liberal theologian Henry Ware Sr., also conducted a boarding school here in the 1830s and 1940s. The house long remained the home of descendants, including Leonard Ware Johnson, who contributed much valuable information about the Allens to the Northborough Historical Society, and Kenneth Myrick, a Tufts University professor and scholar of English Renaissance literature. Finally in 1998, when no Allen descendant could be found to purchase it, the house was sold to someone outside the family for the first time.

Dr. Joseph Allen spent his entire career, from 1816 to 1873, as a clergyman in Northborough, guiding the institution that has evolved into today's Unitarian Church. A course of lectures that he gave at town hall in 1827 marked the beginning of Northborough's version of the lyceum movement. His son Joseph Henry Allen became a Unitarian historian. His son William Allen became the author of popular Latin textbooks.

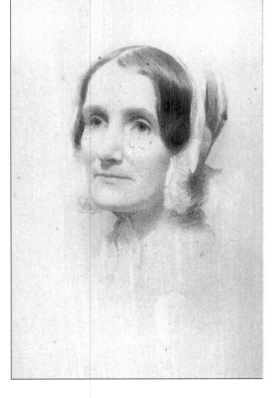

Lucy Clark Ware married Dr. Joseph Allen in 1818, not long after he was settled as town minister. She bore seven children. She also assumed much responsibility in the operation of the Allen School, keeping scrupulous records of the students' progress or, sometimes, the lack of it.

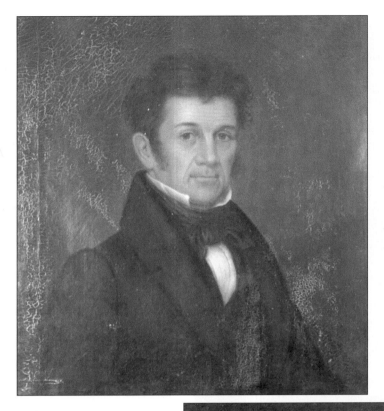

Capt. Cyrus Gale, called thus out of respect for early militia service, settled in Northborough in 1813. He operated a general store on Main Street for more than half a century. An organizer of the Northborough Bank, he also served as town clerk, selectman, assessor, and member of the governor's council. A wealthy philanthropist, Gale died in 1880, just short of his 95th birthday.

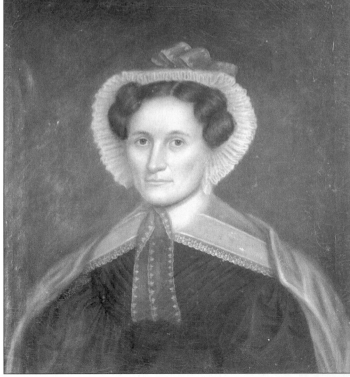

This depiction of Sarah Patrick Gale, the second wife of Capt. Cyrus Gale and the mother of Cyrus Gale Jr., is a companion portrait to that of her husband. The originals were painted c. 1840 by W.R. Wheeler. Both of these oil paintings hang in the Northborough Historical Society museum.

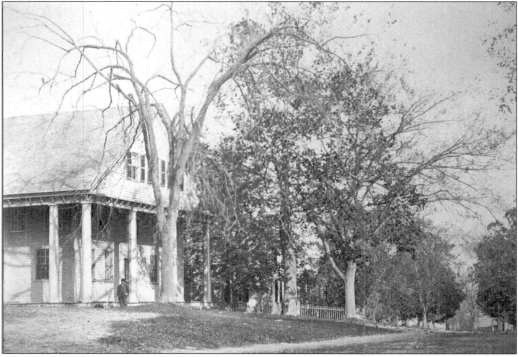

The former Gale store is one of several early-19th-century Greek revival structures on Main Street just east of the town center. Capt. Cyrus Gale sold produce from his 200-acre farm here and also liquor, in the days before the temperance movement changed the attitude of town residents, including that of Gale himself.

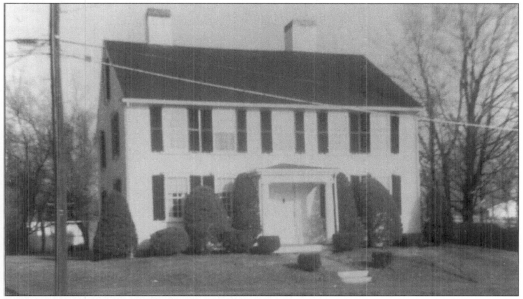

Capt. Cyrus Gale bought this house immediately east of his store in 1824; it remained in the family until 1909. Most of the windows have 24 panes each. In 1991, a widening and straightening project on this part of Main Street cut slightly into the high front lawn seen here, necessitating the construction of a low retaining wall across the front of the property.

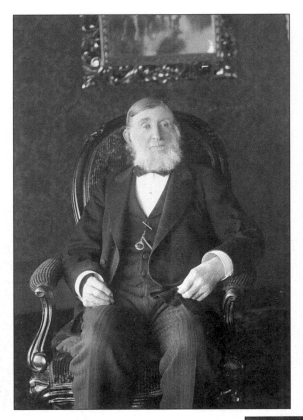

As one of the town's chief benefactors, Cyrus Gale Jr. endowed both the Northborough Free Library building and Assabet Park. He also contributed lavishly to the Gale Fund, which his father had established for the support of indigent townspeople. As his father had, Gale served as a director of the Northborough Bank. He died in 1907 at the age of 83.

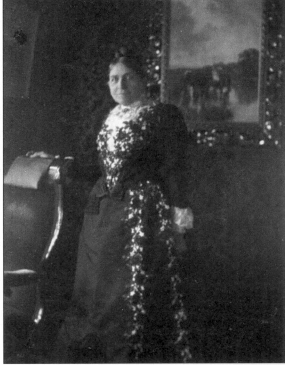

The same picture hangs behind Ellen M. Gale, but her husband's chair has been moved away, and she stands beside one that is no doubt her favorite. She assisted her husband in his many philanthropic deeds and continued in her own right after his death. Among her own gifts to the town was a wrought-iron gate for the Howard Street cemetery.

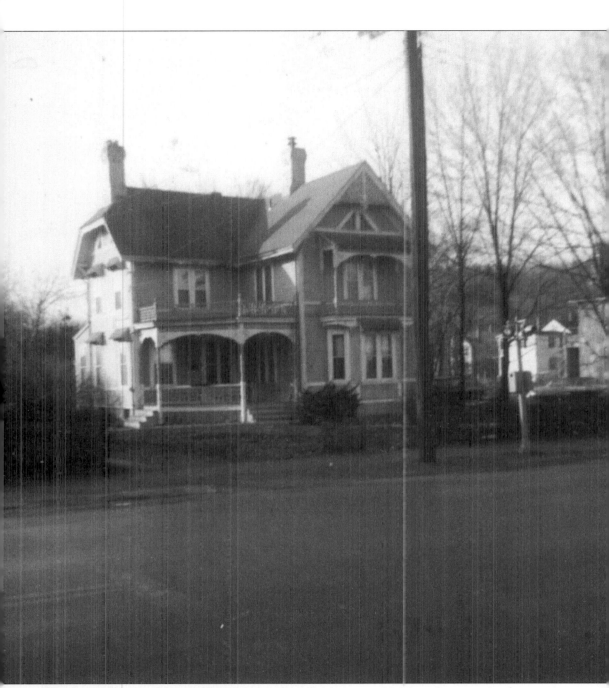

The younger Cyrus Gale and his wife lived in this house at 20 Main Street, near the town center, at the corner of present-day Patty Lane. Several decades younger than his father's house at 43 Main Street, this structure reflects the change toward the style usually called Victorian, even though it preceded the extravagance of late-Victorian architecture. It is interesting that Gale's two main gifts to the town are both near his home: the library, only four doors to the east, and Assabet Park, just two blocks away on South Street. At present, the building at 20 Main Street houses one of Northborough's numerous antique shops, which the proprietor has strategically named after Gale.

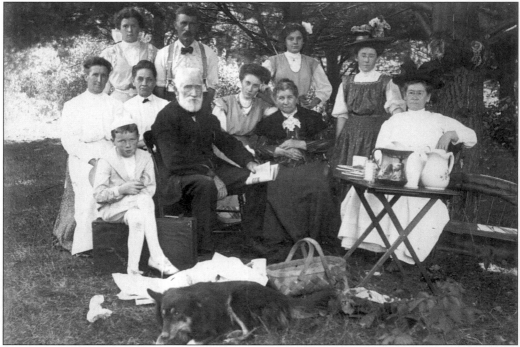

This is a gathering of the Bailey family and intimates, *c.* 1900. David Minor Bailey, a Civil War veteran, was a carpenter by trade but also cultivated an extensive garden. Pictured, from left to right, are the following: (front row) Linus Elliot, David Minor Bailey, Sarah Flagg Bailey, and Carrie Underwood; (middle row) Isabell Bailey, Nellie Elliot, and Hazel Elliot; (back row) Marian Bailey, Eugene Bailey, Charlotte Elliot, and Nellie Underwood.

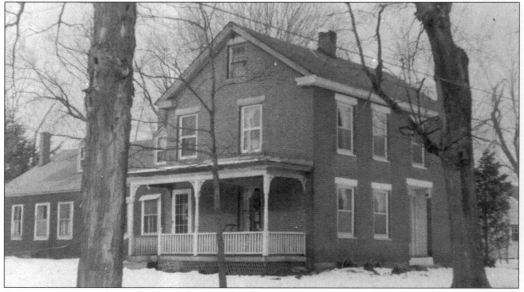

For 70 years, members of the Bailey family called this brick house at 101 Maple Street home. Townspeople referred to the sharp curve in Maple Street at the intersection of Ridge Road, just east of the house, as "Bailey's Corner." Bailey children never had far to walk to school, for all three of the successive 19th-century East School buildings were located nearby.

This bearded gentleman is believed to be Christopher Columbus Eames, a carpenter and carriage maker who came to Northborough from Maine in 1840. In his diary, Eames recorded his work, which also included the doctoring of his neighbors' livestock and in October 1861, his fruitless trip south to search for his son who was missing in action (see pages 19 and 20).

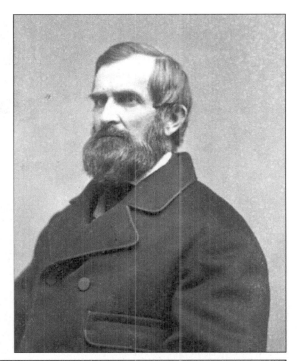

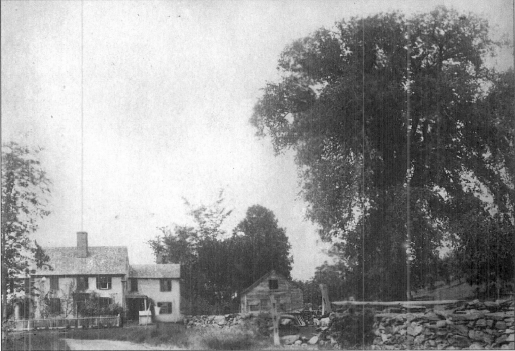

The Columbus Eames farm stood on Main Street one-half mile east of the town center. This farm disappeared in 1882, when Eames sold the acreage to the wealthy firearms manufacturer Daniel Wesson, who wished to build a summer home in Northborough. A short distance east of here, Wesson's older brother had once worked as a gunsmith. Even closer to this site, Wesson's wife, the former Cynthia Hawes, had grown up.

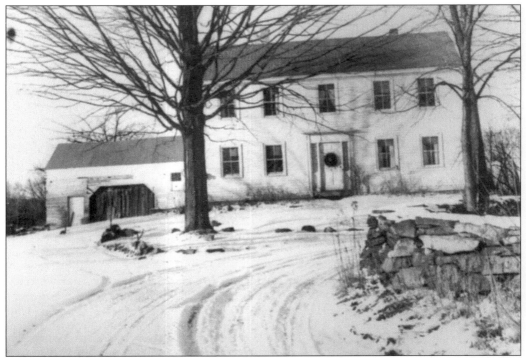

William Babcock built this house in 1752 at what is now 119 Washburn Street. In the 19th century, it became known as the Wright farm. For many years, the property was famed for its peach and cherry trees. It has changed hands many times, but its owners have generally respected its historical character.

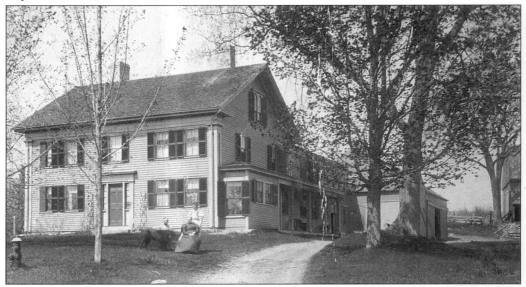

The 1752 Samuel Gamwell Jr. house at 6 Lancaster Road, off Whitney Street, belonged to the Coreys in 1897. Seated in front of the house are Edwin Corey and his aunt Sarah. Standing behind them is Corey's wife, Delia Corey, who assiduously collected information about her home from previous dwellers. Much is therefore known about its appearance well back in the 19th century.

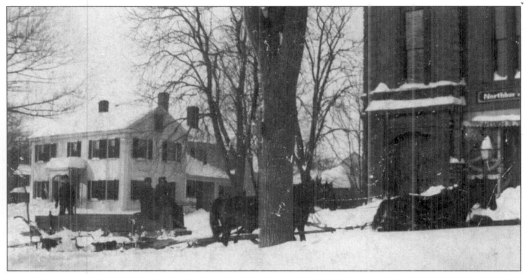

The Crossley house, standing immediately west of the old town hall, gave charm to the town center for years. As the Spa and later as the Whitehouse Donut Shop, it became a favorite hangout of several generations of townspeople. Today, the Central Café serves a similar function, occupying the same site in a small shopping plaza that displaced the Crossley house in the early 1960s.

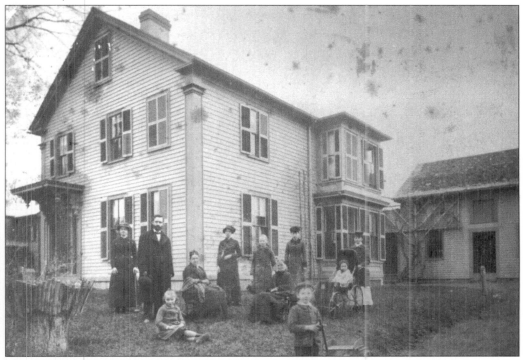

The family and connections of the Reverend Edward L. Chute range across the lawn of the Evangelical Congregational church parsonage. The church acquired the property at 55 Main Street in 1875 and retained it as a parsonage until shortly after World War II. Chute served at the church from 1885 to 1896. Judging from the size of his immediate family, this image dates from the later part of his ministry.

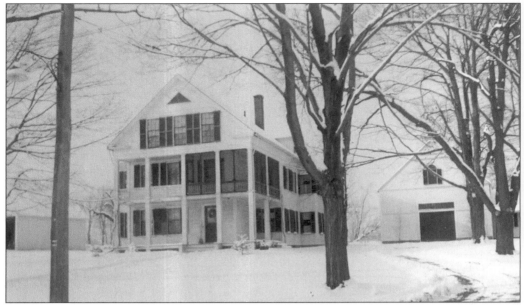

After former Northborough High School classmates Jennie Morse and Philip Hilliard (see page 110) married in 1897, they lived in this house at 23 Whitney Street. Their daughter Elizabeth Hilliard, after retiring from her position as a high school history teacher in Attleboro, returned here to live while she enjoyed another career as librarian of the Northborough Free Library from 1953 to 1964. She appears in the cover photograph.

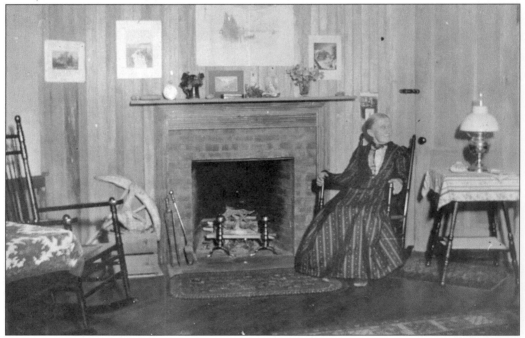

Philip Hilliard's mother, Harriet Hilliard, is pictured here in a summer cottage in Owl's Head, Maine, c. 1900. She and her daughter Carolyn spent the summer months enjoying temperate weather, viewing the ocean, visiting with friends and acquaintances, dining, picking blueberries, and writing letters home to the family.

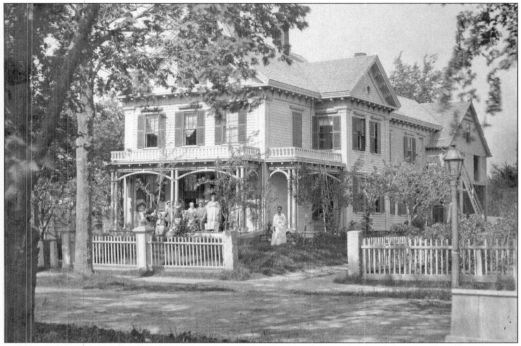

The John Stone house dates from c. 1850. Members of the family are gathered for this photograph, which apparently dates from the 1890s. The house, despite modifications, is still recognizable at 10 Church Street. It was the longtime home of R. Gordon Walker, a Northborough selectman in the 1930s and 1940s, and his wife, Florence Walker. Today, the house is a tearoom.

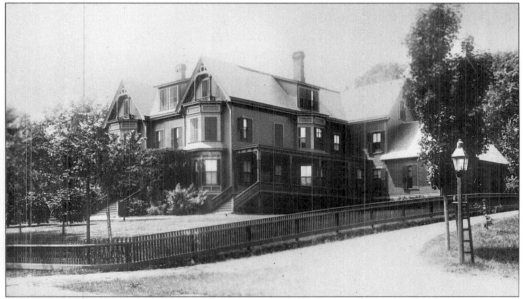

David Wood built this handsome dwelling across the road from his Hudson Street mill (see page 82) in the 1880s, when both entrepreneurs and employees often lived within a few steps of the workplace. It is another of the notable Northborough buildings that fell victim to fires. Today, a utilitarian but decidedly unprepossessing electrical transfer station sits on the lot.

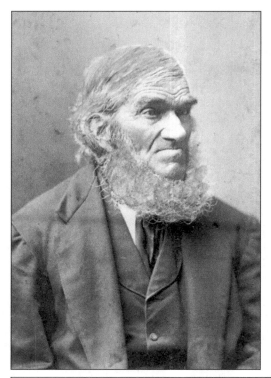

Jairus Lincoln came to Northborough in 1844 and conducted a boarding school, which apparently inherited the students of Dr. Joseph Allen, his brother-in-law. Lincoln also composed music, including antislavery hymns, as he fiercely opposed slavery and probably did much to fan the abolitionist flame in Northborough in the 1840s. His granddaughter Amy Barnes married Prof. Samuel Maynard (see page 56).

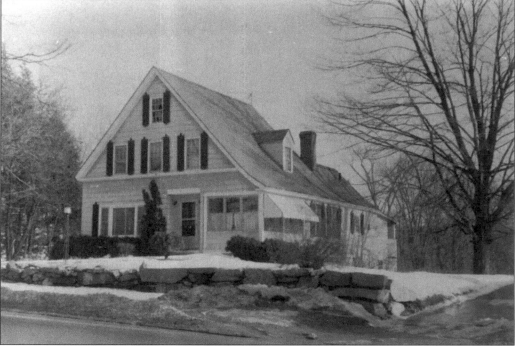

Rev. Samuel Ashley lived in this house, the present 100 Main Street, after returning from post–Civil War religious and educational work in several southern states. Priscilla LaPorte, who appears on page 115 as one of the high school basketball players, grew up in this house from 1911 through the 1920s. Her mother, Alice Hinds LaPorte, appears on page 84.

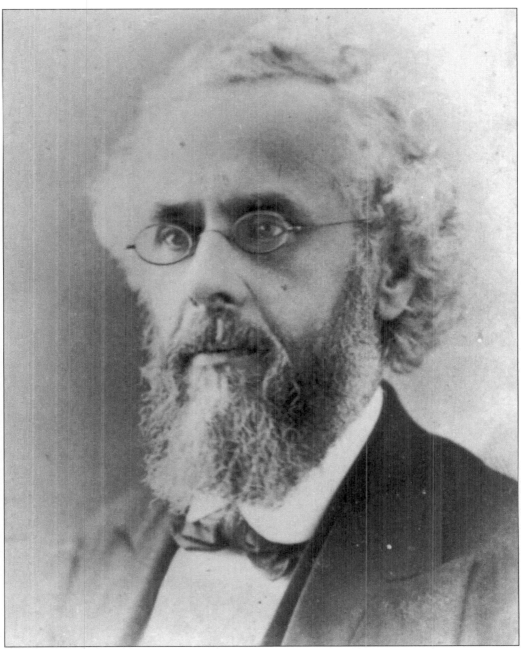

Resigning his position in the Evangelical Congregational church in 1864 to devote himself to missionary work in the South, Samuel Ashley established an orphanage and a school in North Carolina. In 1868, he was named the superintendent of public instruction for that state, but his determination to provide educational opportunities for freed African Americans displeased his critics. In 1871, he moved to New Orleans to head Straight University, an American Missionary Association institution for black students. He later served as pastor of a black Congregational church in Atlanta. Ashley returned to Northborough in 1878 and became, of all things, its postmaster, while continuing his educational activity as chairman of the school committee. This remarkable man died in 1887 at the age of 68.

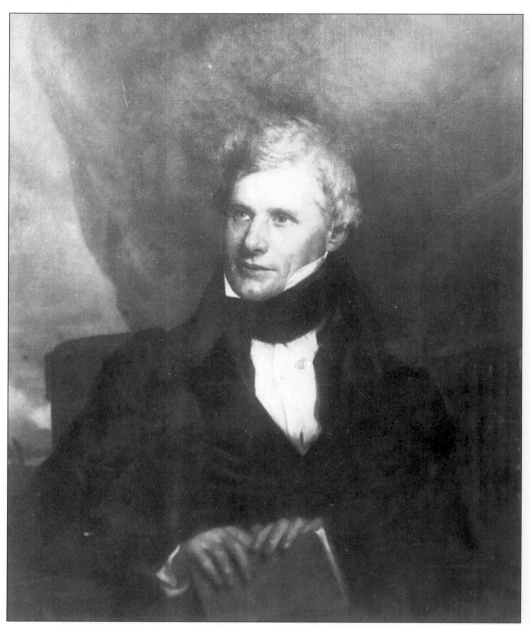

It was probably during one of his terms as governor of Massachusetts in the early 1840s that John Davis sat for this portrait by the prominent painter Francis Alexander. When Davis was born in 1787, his father, Isaac Davis, operated a tannery in the southern part of town. Although other family members kept this business going until almost the end of the 19th century, Davis opted for higher education. He graduated with high honors from Yale in 1812 and began a long legal and political career. In addition to several one-year terms as governor, he served as a member of both houses of Congress. Although not an abolitionist, Davis's strong opposition to the expansion of slavery during his term as a U.S. senator was instrumental in the passage of the famous Wilmot Proviso, which outlawed the extension of slavery into any territory gained through negotiations aimed at ending the Mexican War. This portrait hangs in the Northborough Historical Society museum.

Noah Wadsworth poses in 1883, two years before he succeeded his father, John Wadsworth, as proprietor of the grocery store in Page's Block in the middle of town (see page 16). The business remained J. Wadsworth & Company until Wadsworth's death in 1922. His widow married Dr. Josiah Stanley, but she lived only a few months thereafter.

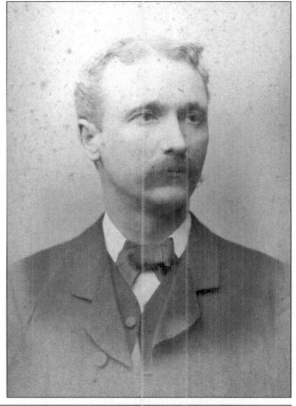

Noah Wadsworth's great passion was horses, and he seldom owned fewer than a half dozen. Oddly, Wadsworth for many years owned no more land than the half-acre Main Street lot on which his house and barn stood. Long after this early picture was taken, he finally purchased a pasture lot.

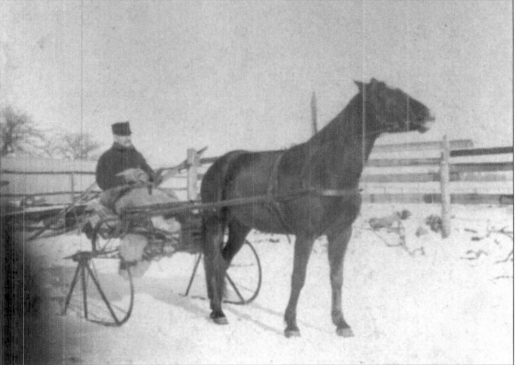

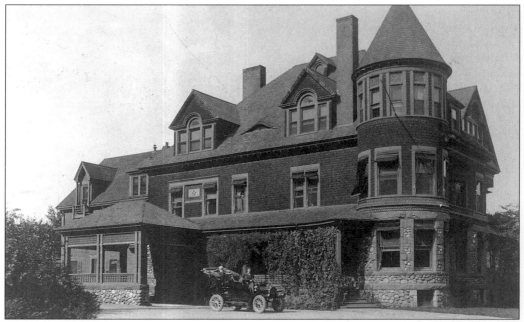

Outside his mansion on Hudson Street, Ezra Chapin perches in one of Northborough's early automobiles. From 1855 to 1862, Chapin prospected for gold in California. However, it was the cotton mill he inherited from his father that paid for his mansion. The woman in this photograph dating from the first decade of the 20th century is unidentified.

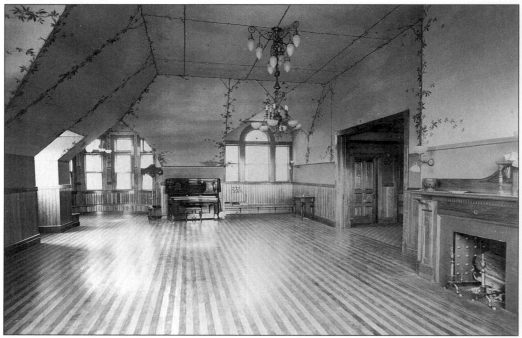

The Chapins imported a landscape photographer from Portland, Maine, to take this picture of their upstairs ballroom; its glory was relatively short-lived. On March 26, 1915, some 25 years after being constructed, the mansion was destroyed in a fire accidentally set off by carpenters doing renovations.

As the wife of a prosperous mill owner, it fell to Ellen Chapin to be a leading hostess; she appears fit for the role. Born as Ellen Frances Cooper in Charlestown, she married Ezra Chapin in 1864, at about the time he became his father's partner in the mill.

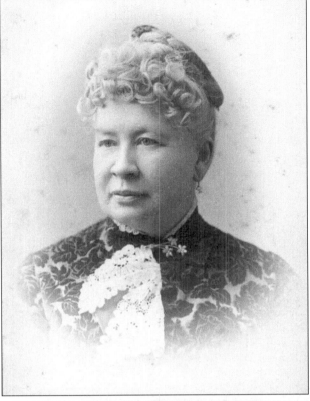

Ezra Chapin proceeds from his home along Hudson Street toward town, riding in a traditional form of transportation. He raised horses as an avocation and entered some of them in trotting races in nearby Worcester—but not for the money. His interest was an amateur one in the purest sense of the term: he loved horses.

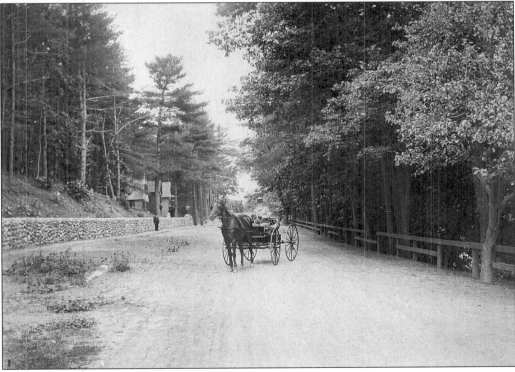

Amy Barnes, an early graduate of the Boston Woman's Institute (later, a part of the Massachusetts Institute of Technology) married Samuel T. Maynard. She was a teacher and civic leader who founded the Amherst Woman's Club and served as its first president. In her eighties, she agitated tirelessly for the establishment and development of the United Nations. She died at age 90 in 1949.

Though not born in Northborough, Samuel T. Maynard sprang from an old Northborough family and spent much of his life here. As a professor of botany at Massachusetts Agricultural College (now the University of Massachusetts at Amherst), he wrote extensively on horticultural subjects and prepared several exhibits for the 1893 Columbian Exposition in Chicago. Retiring in 1902, he settled permanently in town but continued to write and lecture.

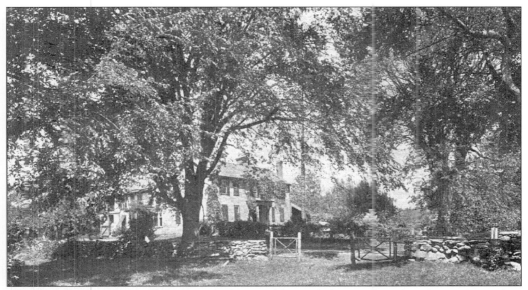

The present-day 130 South Street was the Northborough home of Prof. and Mrs. Samuel T. Maynard after his retirement. Following his death in 1923, Amy Maynard operated it as a summer guest house, calling it the "Homestead." For a consideration of $12 to $15 per week, she offered her guests "the pleasures of country life and the simple atmosphere of a home."

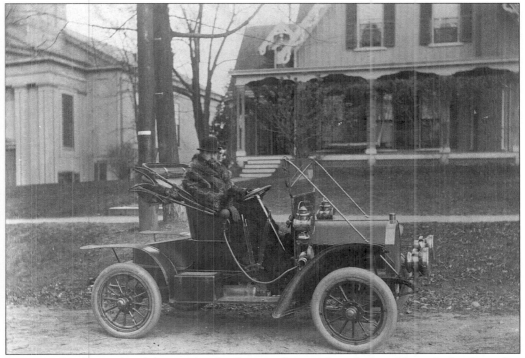

Ensconced in his automobile—said to be the town's second, with Ezra Chapin's the first—Dr. Josiah Stanley parks in front of the Victorian home owned by Noah and Almira Wadsworth. A town physician for 51 years, Stanley lived with the Wadsworths (see page 53) and inherited the house after Wadsworth's death in 1923. Stanley continued to live there until he died in 1940. The house stood immediately east of Trinity Church; the site is now a parking lot.

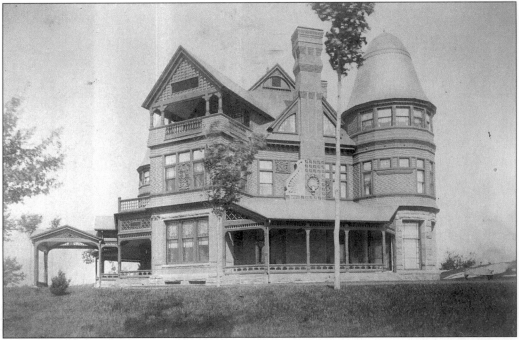

In 1882, Daniel B. Wesson, a partner in the firearms manufacturing firm of Smith & Wesson, began to construct this elaborate summer home one-half mile east of the center of Northborough. He called it the Cliffs. From its stained-glass skylight to its parquet oak floors, it is a spectacular mansion, which reportedly cost Wesson $300,000. Around the middle of the 20th century, it became a restaurant called the White Cliffs.

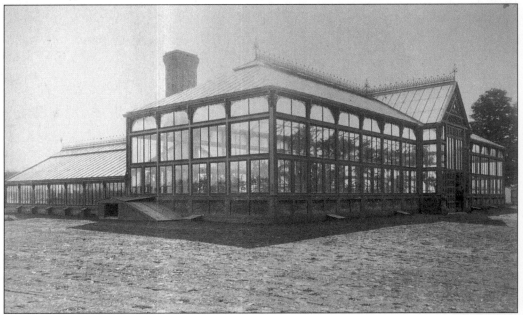

At the corner of Main and Maple Streets across the road from his mansion, Daniel B. Wesson built this greenhouse, obviously large enough to house good-sized trees. In the late 1920s, the greenhouse was purchased by a florist from Framingham, who removed it from the site.

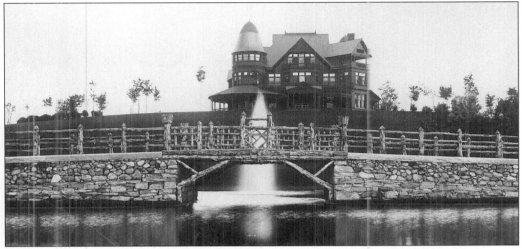

Daniel B. Wesson created this little pond with its ornate bridge west of his mansion. He achieved this by drawing water from the Bartlett Pond runoff, pumping it to a cistern on top of a nearby hill, and then piping it for nearly a mile. Today, the pond is long gone; an upscale housing development has occupied this part of the estate since the early 1990s.

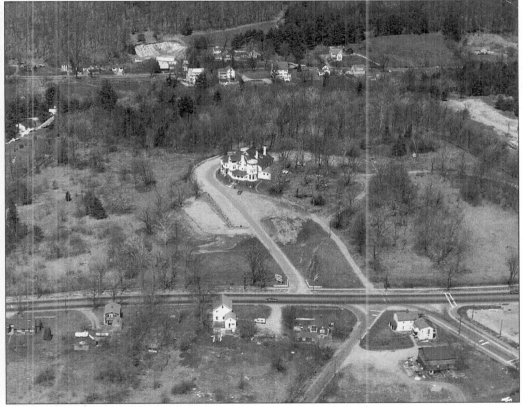

In 1965, the Wesson mansion looked like this from the air. It had by this time acquired several boxlike additions built to satisfy the needs of the White Cliffs restaurant, which it had become. The Assabet River, which bounds the property on the north, flows unseen between Hudson Street, near the top of the photograph, and the line of trees below

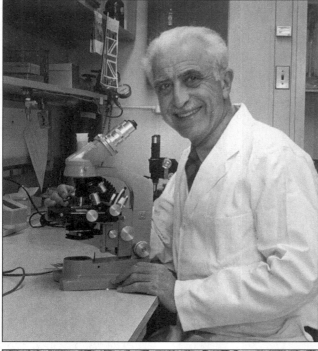

Gregory Goodwin Pincus, together with Hudson Hoagland, established the Worcester Foundation for Experimental Biology (now the Worcester Foundation for Biomedical Research). In the 1950s, Pincus and his associates at the foundation developed the first practical birth control pill and thus brought about a social revolution, the effects of which are still difficult to estimate. (Photograph courtesy of Worcester Foundation for Biomedical Research.)

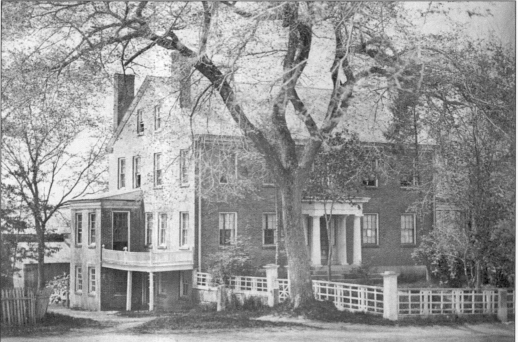

Gregory Pincus lived in this house at 30 Main Street, which was constructed in an early-19th-century Federal style using bricks from local brickyards. Dr. Stephen Ball III, the son of the doctor who lived two doors away (see pages 32 and 33), lived in Boston but built the house as a summer residence. Today, the building holds a commercial enterprise that has respected its historical integrity.

Rev. Charles S. Pease was pastor of Northborough's original Baptist Church twice. He first served from 1903 to 1910. Then, after serving at several other churches, he became pastor again from 1922 until his retirement in 1934. Like several other Northborough ministers, he pursued historical research; two of his topics were Luther Rice (see page 23) and area Native American history.

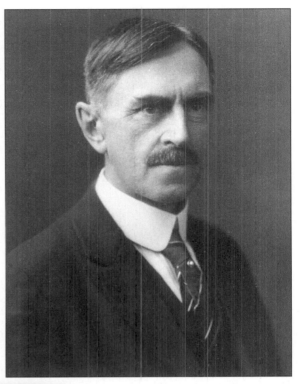

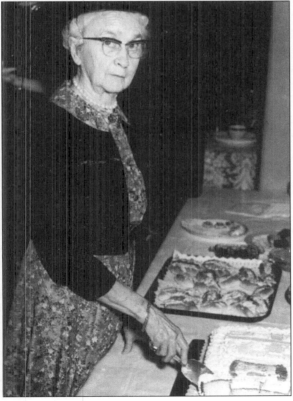

As a young woman, Alice Bowes Brigham taught music at Northborough schools, played the organ in various area churches, and directed many musical programs in town. (She appears as a student on page 106.) In her later years, as Alice Kimball, she served as president of the Northborough Historical Society. She was also the organization's first curator and an industrious and productive historical researcher. She died in 1973 at age 96.

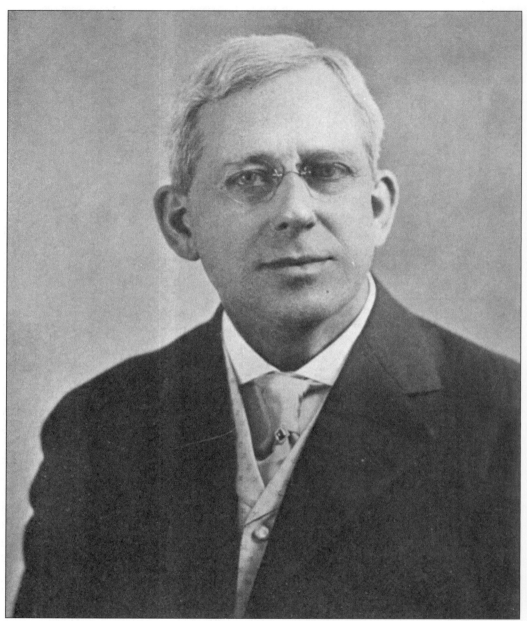

Rev. Josiah Coleman Kent came to the First Church in 1895 and soon demonstrated not only ministerial devotion but a voracious appetite for town history. In addition to publishing the first comprehensive history of the town in 1921, his final year in town, he was the author of two other important historical records. His *Journal of the First Congregational Church and Society of Northborough, Massachusetts* details his ministry. His *Current Events Journal* catches the life of the town in the decade from 1911 to 1920, at a time when few perceived the value of a record of everyday happenings. Unfortunately, he inspired no imitators. As a result, historical researchers find the next few decades of Northborough life more shadowy. Kent was also the chief motivating force behind the establishment of the Northborough Historical Society in 1906. He served faithfully as its secretary for 15 years thereafter. His *Northborough History* remains the most thorough account by far of the development of the town up to his time.

Edwin W. Proctor stands outside his home at 154 Whitney Street. As a teacher of French at the Choate School, he instructed young Joseph Kennedy Jr. and and his brother John Kennedy. In 1967, around the time of this photograph, Proctor gave the town a 75-acre tract, Edmund Hill Woods, for recreational purposes. His many contributions to the Northborough Historical Society include the building that today houses the society's archive.

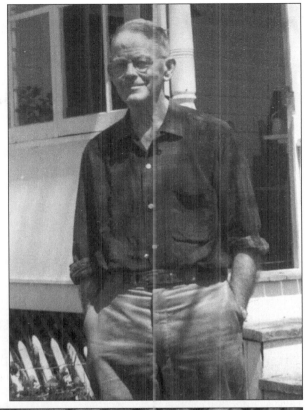

Edwin Proctor's grandfather bought the house in 1870 from the Carruth family, who owned considerable acreage in this part of town as far back as the mid-18th century. Horatio Carruth built the house and barn from wood cut on nearby Edmund Hill. Carruth Drive, a nearby cul-de-sac, exemplifies the town's habit of naming streets for prominent early settlers.

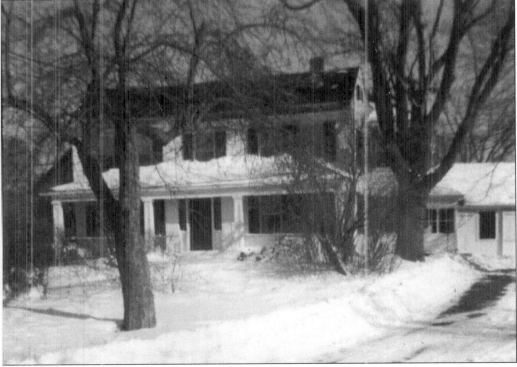

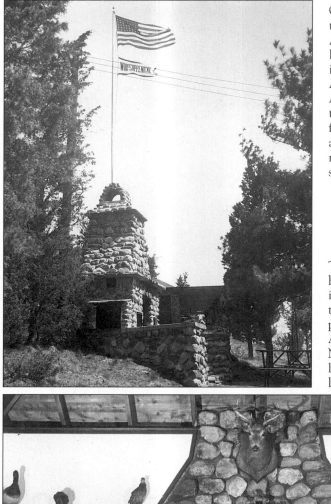

On a hill above Howard Street in the northern part of town, Walter A. Mentzer built this hunting lodge of fieldstone in 1909, calling it Whipsuppenicke, a Native American tribal name. In 1941, Albert and Vera Green purchased the lodge, but after living there for 11 years, they dismantled it and built a new, larger, and more modern Whipsuppenicke on the same hilltop.

The Native American and hunting motifs are well-illustrated in this photograph of a room from the lodge. Walter Mentzer clearly prized the art of taxidermy. Although he was a member of a Northborough family, Mentzer lived in Boston and used his stone lodge simply as a country retreat.

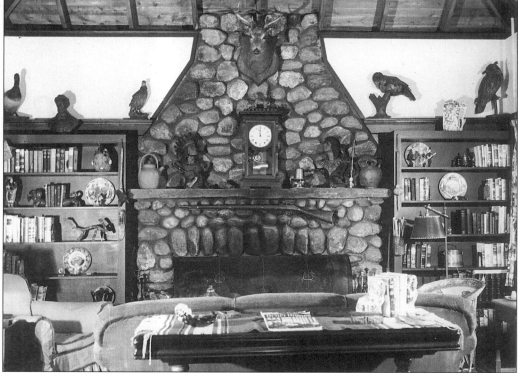

Three
GETTING AROUND

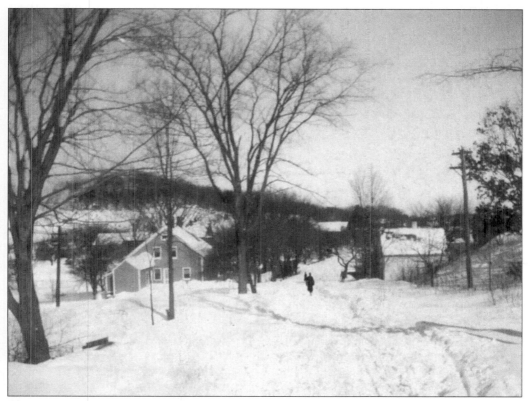

This winter picture captures a portion of Hudson Street northeastward from its intersection with Pierce Street. The smooth surface to the left is the ice of Wallace's Pond, which is formed by a dam on Cold Harbor Brook near its confluence with the Assabet River, flowing out of sight to the right of Hudson Street. The time appears to be the early 20th century.

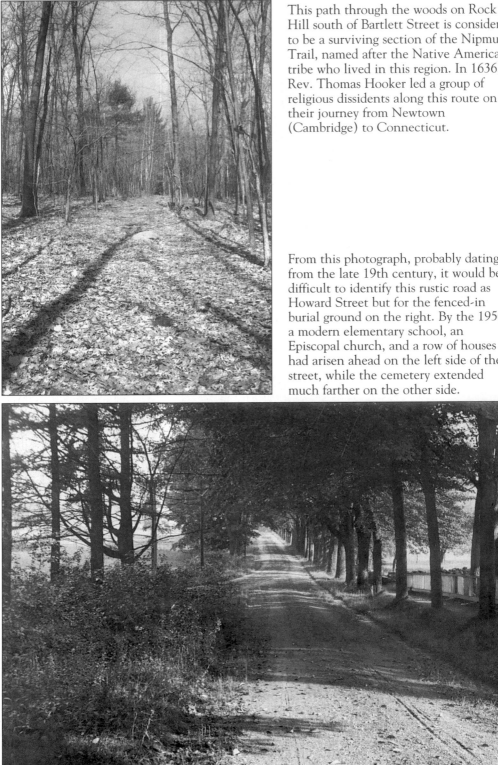

This path through the woods on Rock Hill south of Bartlett Street is considered to be a surviving section of the Nipmuc Trail, named after the Native American tribe who lived in this region. In 1636, Rev. Thomas Hooker led a group of religious dissidents along this route on their journey from Newtown (Cambridge) to Connecticut.

From this photograph, probably dating from the late 19th century, it would be difficult to identify this rustic road as Howard Street but for the fenced-in burial ground on the right. By the 1950s, a modern elementary school, an Episcopal church, and a row of houses had arisen ahead on the left side of the street, while the cemetery extended much farther on the other side.

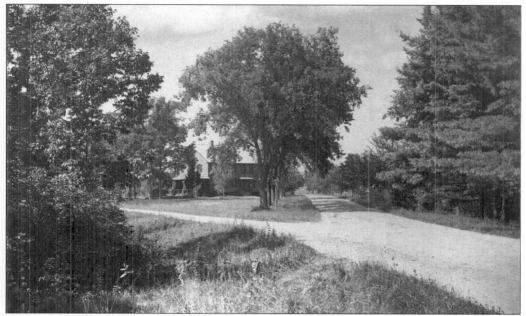

Not until recently has the Pleasant Street and Church Street intersection—a familiar sight to generations of residents—been reconfigured to force motorists to a full stop. Church Street is now one of the busiest in town. The building half hidden behind the trees is the first Evangelical Congregational church (1832), a private residence for many years now.

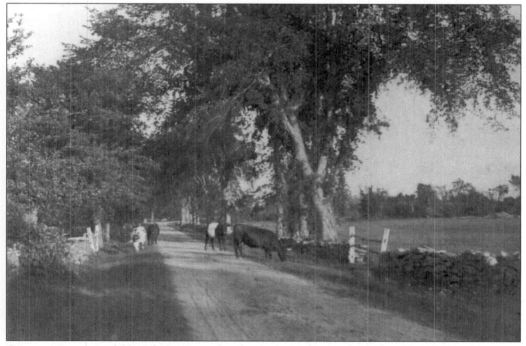

Cows occupy part of Church Street, today the main artery into town from Interstate I-290. The view probably faces east, and the intersection on the right is probably West Street. Both the Holloway house (the Williams house in the late 19th century—see page 24) and the West School (see page 107) stand just out of sight on the left.

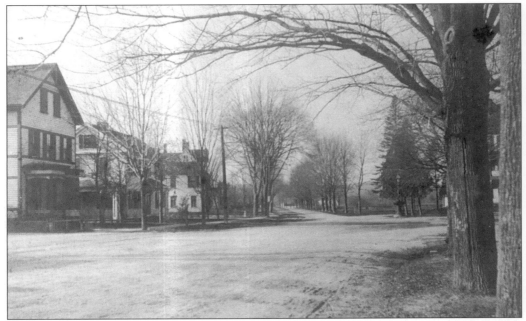

Little in this 1899 view of West Main Street, taken from the center of town, remains today. Church Street flares to the right. Of the houses on the left, the first two—formerly Nos. 27 and 31, just west of the present Lowe's Store—survived until 1979. The third house, now a storage building for a retailer across the street, has been modified.

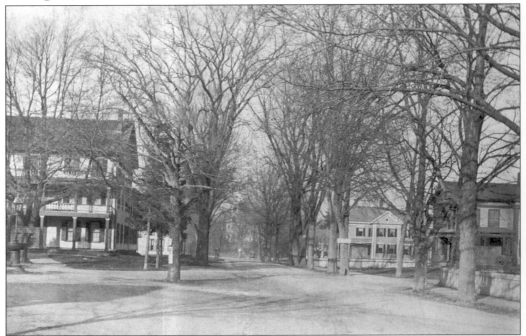

From Main Street in the tranquil Northborough of *c.* 1900, Church Street is visible as far its westward turn, where the Unitarian church stands on its eminence. The corner building on the left is the Northborough Hotel (see page 14). J.T. Fay lived at the corner house on the right; the one beyond is the John Stone house (see page 49).

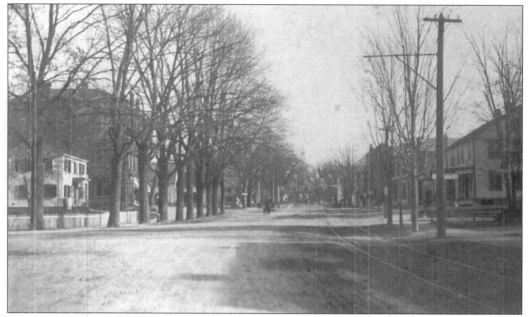

The only vehicle in this eastward view of the town center is horse drawn. However, the trolley tracks and electric light poles signal the technological revolution that was beginning to transform town centers, rendering locations such as the one that this photographer occupies increasingly hazardous in the years to come. The large building on the left is the 1868 town hall.

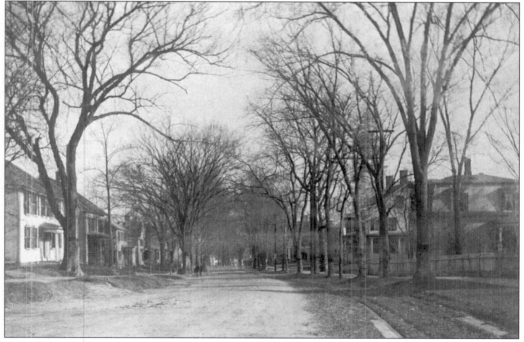

A little farther east, and still looking eastward, Main Street offers a series of older houses. The photographer is standing in front of the library or Dr. Stephen Ball's house. The first house on the right, at 42 Main Street with the mansard roof, has changed little. Capt. Cyrus Gale's house (see page 41) is in the left foreground. There are, of course, fewer trees in this area today.

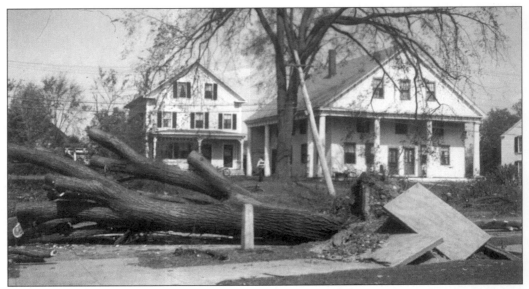

From a vantage point in front of the library, the photographer turns his camera north across Main Street to catch the destruction from the 1938 hurricane. The large tree is not merely broken but also uprooted. The building to the right is the former Gale store, long since converted to apartments.

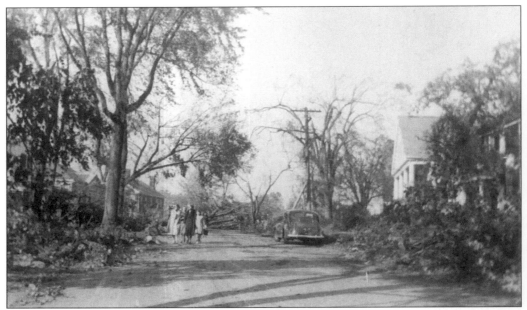

Several women walking east on Main Street survey the devastation left by the hurricane. One person was killed by a tree falling on an automobile in front of the library, which can barely be seen at the left. This photograph was taken from almost the same spot as the winter view from an earlier era on the next page.

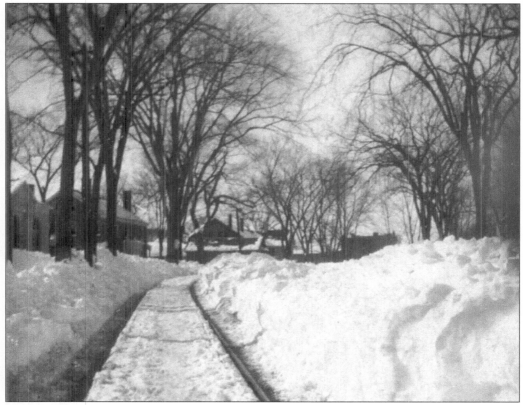

A few hundred yards east of the center of town, only the trolley has apparently been making it through the snowbanks. At the extreme left, the Northborough Free Library is visible. The large house just beyond it was home to a succession of doctors over the years. Several decades after this picture was taken, Dr. Gregory Pincus lived in the house (see page 60).

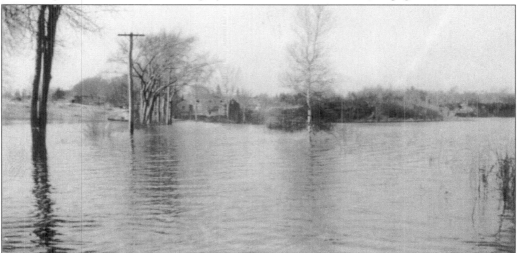

Heavy rain and melting snow caused severe flooding in the late winter of 1936. From relatively high ground on School Street, an observer turns the camera northward to capture the overflow of the Assabet River. Usually only a few yards wide, the stream rose above its banks on March 12, 1936.

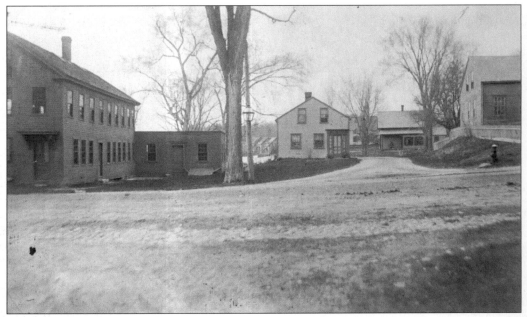

Of these four structures at Main and River Streets in the 1890s, only the factory on the left—where Milo Hildreth's workers made ornamental combs—failed to survive until the 1990s. The house in the middle was later rotated 90 degrees and inserted between the other two houses to permit the straightening of River Street. Part of the Capt. Samuel Wood house can be seen at the right (see page 31).

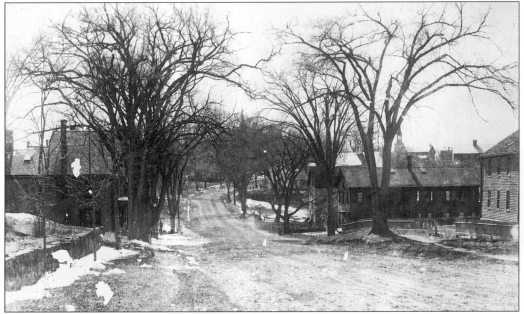

Looking west from Main Street, some of the same buildings are visible; the date, however, is years earlier. The Capt. Samuel Wood house is at the extreme right. Visible over the top of the Hildreth factory building is the steeple of the Evangelical Congregational church (later Trinity Church). The stone retaining wall on the left remains today, as do miles of stone walls in all parts of town.

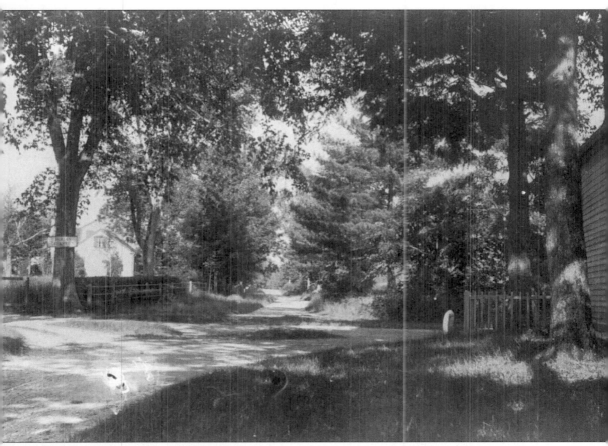

Probably few townspeople today will recognize this intersection. The house that can be seen in part at the extreme right still stands at the corner of Winter and Whitney Streets. The latter street, as the sign indicates, points the traveler north to Berlin and Clinton. At the time of this 1880s photograph, the house on the opposite corner, now gone, belonged to John Minot Rice, who was a mathematics professor at the U.S. Naval Academy. Standing once in the triangle formed by Church and Pleasant Streets, the building had housed one of the oldest schools in town, the Northborough Seminary. In 1807, Rice's father had it moved to the corner of Whitney at Rice Avenue, as the street opposite Winter Street was later called. For a number of years in the 20th century, the Rice house served as a nursing home. It was razed in the early 1970s.

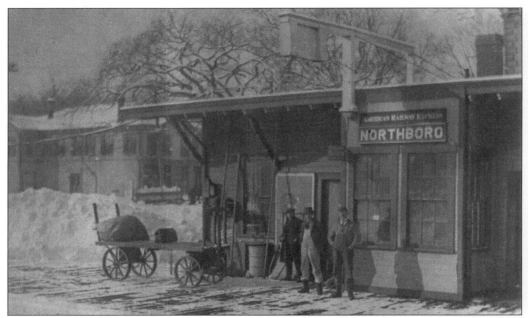

Harry J. England, right, is seen early in his career as a Northborough station agent, which lasted from 1900 to 1943. England's granddaughter Mildred Sanders remembers accompanying him as he pushed a loaded handcar along the tracks from the main station to Talbot Station, farther south. She relates that when he heard a train approaching, he simply lifted the handcar from the tracks until it passed. Freight trains still rumble through Northborough, but passenger service is long gone.

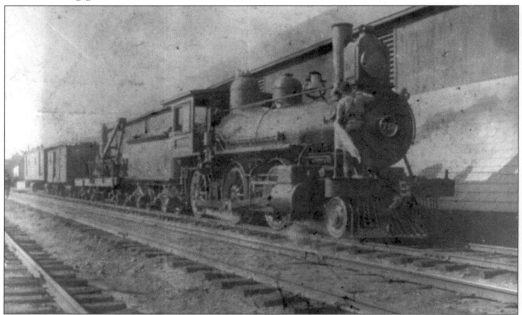

The railroad came to Northborough in 1853. By the time photography became widespread, trains were such common sights that they were infrequent subjects. The perspective for this photograph of a work train is east of the tracks and somewhat south of Pierce Street. The structure behind the train, a coal trestle, was blown over in the 1938 hurricane.

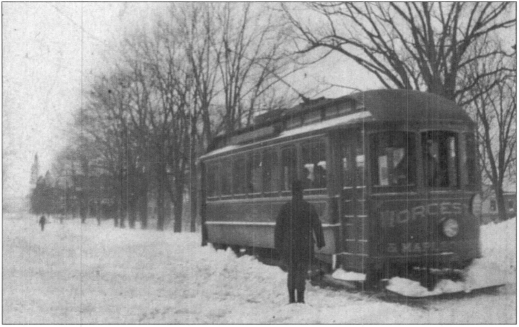

Car No. 25 was one of the original cars purchased at the inception of the Worcester and Marlborough Street Railway in 1897. It is bound for Marlborough on a winter day. The photograph was probably taken before 1900 but after the winter of 1898, when there would have been no sense in the man's boarding just west of the track (see the next caption).

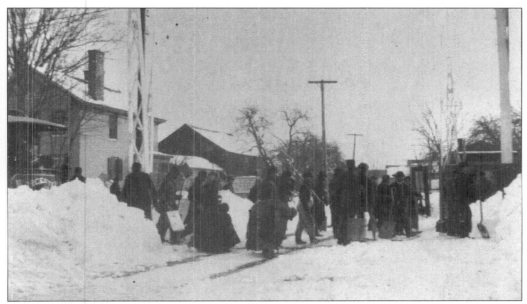

What are these people doing? They have reached the end of the line in their westward-bound open-platform car and must now cross the New Haven Railroad tracks on foot to continue their journey on another car. For a few months after the trolley began operating, railroad officials refused to permit streetcars to cut into their right-of-way. Note the crossing tender's shanty on the right.

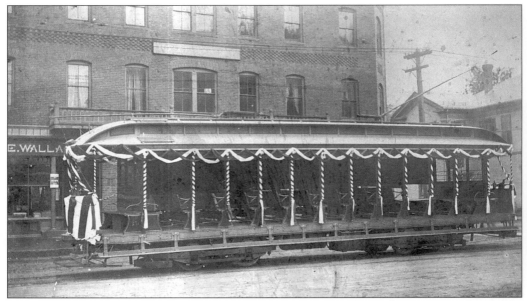

On Main Street, a trolley car is at rest. Through most of the trolley's 28-year history in Northborough, Wallace's meat market occupied quarters in the Winn-Whitaker building, but the electric light poles place this picture no earlier than 1908. This Worcester Consolidated Railway's 14-bench open car appears to have come from Worcester, but the benches are set up for passengers to face west.

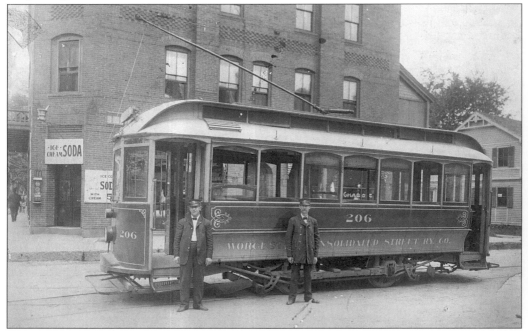

This car was built by Jackson and Sharp in Wilmington, Delaware, in 1890. This rare picture of a trolley car on the Westborough–Northborough line, however, was taken after 1900. Behind the car is the South Street face of the Winn-Whitaker building. The mortar and pestle over the door of the corner store indicate the pharmacy of Seth Emery, but the only signs in sight advertise sodas.

Four

AT WORK

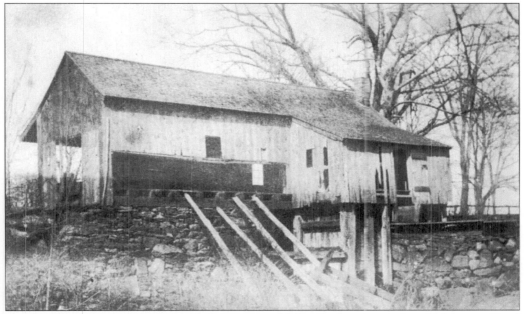

In 1672, the Massachusetts General Court granted John Brigham more than 200 acres of land in what is now Northborough in return for services rendered as a surveyor. As the first known white settler within the limits of the town, Brigham built a sawmill on Howard Brook near the Whitney Street crossing. This is a later mill at the same site.

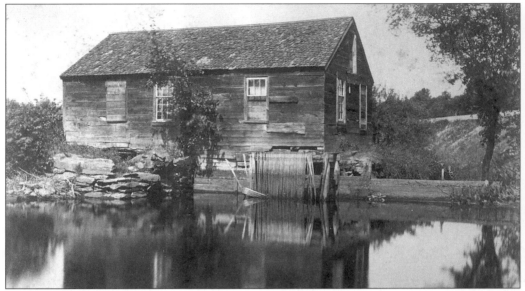

Why was this now-defunct building, photographed *c.* 1880, called the Toad Mill? One theory was that it looked like a toad. It stood on Howard Brook east of Whitney Street. In 1839, Bush & Haynes—the first of several local comb-making establishments—occupied it. Today, a candle factory flourishes on the site.

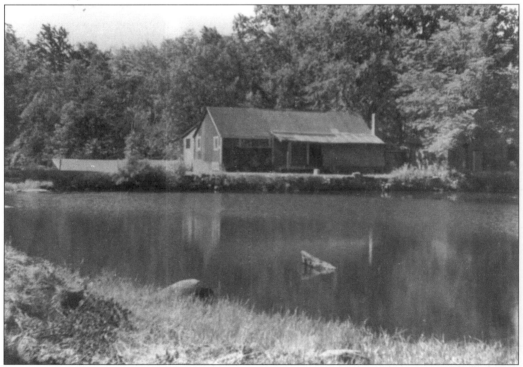

Shown is the Toren cider mill on Cold Harbor Brook at Crawford Street. Benzoin Tartakovsky was a Russian immigrant whose wife, Leah, simplified the family name to Toren when they were married, although he did not change his surname legally for years thereafter. The couple settled in Northborough *c.* 1920 and for the next 40 years, their cider was prized for its quality.

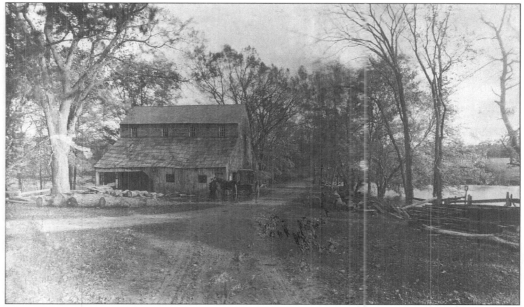

The superstructure of the Smith Mill on Otis Street eventually gave way to a building that housed the Armeno Cereal Company, manufacturers of the bulgur wheat cereal that was dear to those of Armenian heritage. Today, another member of the same family roasts, blends, and sells coffee from around the world at the mill site.

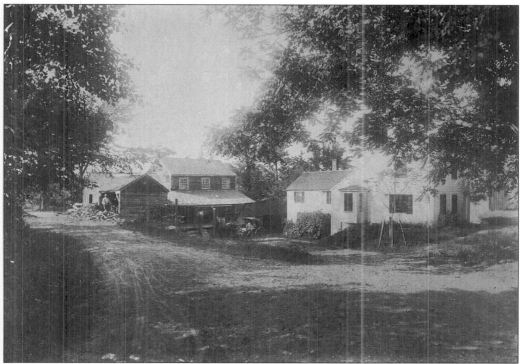

At the foot of Mill Street stands a mill that was known by the names of its several owners; Lt. John Martyn, son of the first town minister, was one of the earliest owners. This facility was last used by the Proctor Lumber Company in the early 20th century. It was torn down in 1958.

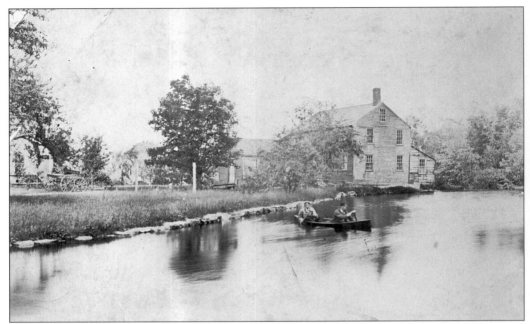

This mill pond remains, somewhat diminished, near the center of town, and no canoeists have been seen paddling on it lately. The mill pictured here is usually referred to as the Gibson Mill, after another of Northborough's comb makers. It stood behind what is today the building at 2 Whitney Street.

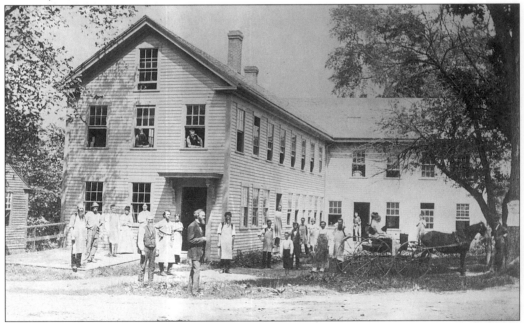

The southwest corner of Main and River Streets has been home to innumerable enterprises over the years. Among the products that have been made or sold at this site are cameras, paint, and motorcycles. Milo Hildreth and his employees gathered outside his comb factory for this c. 1890 photograph. Between the railing at the left and the building beyond, the Assabet River flows.

Workers are preparing to remove a huge elm tree from in front of 75 Main Street in 1912. The next two buildings on the left are long gone, as is the light-colored structure opposite. The dark building, which still stands, then housed Ed Smith's bone mill. Just beyond it, a railing marks the Assabet River bridge. Tree warden Tarble Haskell stands between the pole and the tree.

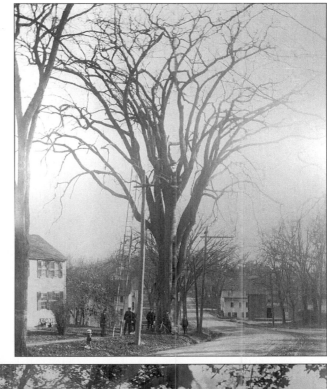

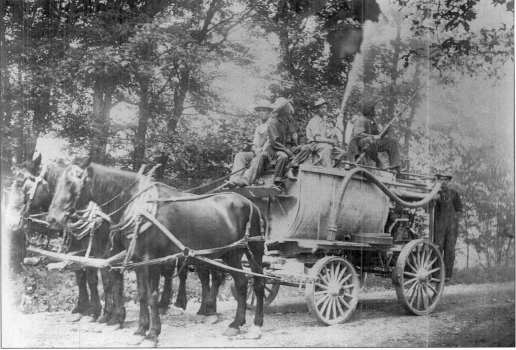

This depiction of tree sprayers c. 1915 recalls the era before the publication of Rachel Carson's *Silent Spring*, when public works departments had no idea of the long-term damage done by pesticides. The sprayers are, from left to right, unidentified, William Warren, Tarble Haskell, unidentified, and Everett Blakely.

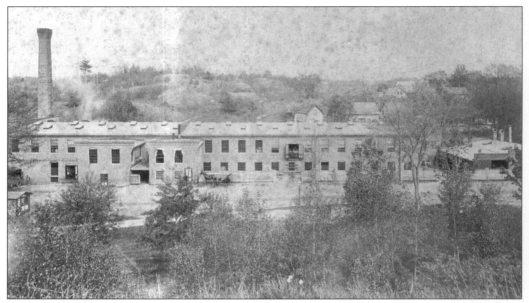

Rivaling the Chapin Mill (see page 85) as a seat of industry, David Wood's woolen mill at Hudson and Allen Streets had already survived several fires by the time he erected this brick building in 1888, not long before this photograph was taken. After the decline of milling, the building housed a maker of church furniture. It also housed Basketville, a well-known New England retailer, before its conversion into condominiums in the late 1980s.

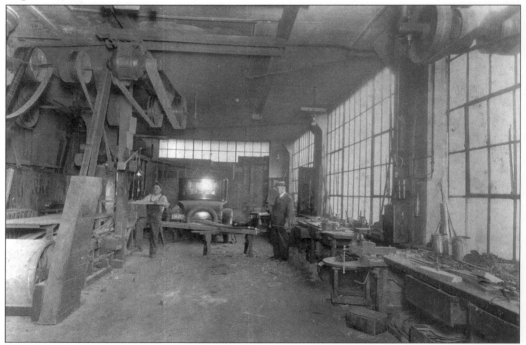

From the late 1930s to the late 1960s, Richard Butler headed Gothic Craft, a business that made pews, altars, and other church furnishings in the old Wood Mill. Much of the equipment was antiquated, but the factory attracted skilled artisans and did superior work. An offshoot of the company continues to operate in London, Kentucky.

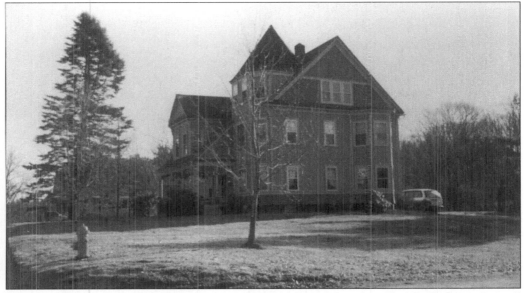

Henry M. Francis designed this house for Northborough comb maker Walter M. Farwell in 1893. It stands at 120 Hudson Street, a short distance from Farwell's factory. The present owners have reversed a trend of neglect that this handsome dwelling had suffered in previous decades.

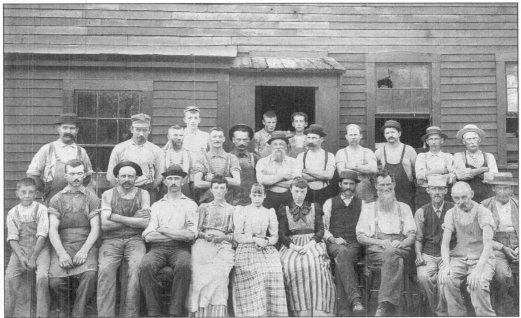

Walter M. Farwell's comb-making factory employed some two dozen people c. 1896. Posing are, from left to right, the following: (front row) unidentified, Fred Garfield, Frank Burbank, Albert Farwell, Agnes Garrity, Alice Harrington, Jennie Lewis, owner Walter M. Farwell, Alonzo Farwell, Fred Twichell, Charles Lowe, and Gilbar Comtois; (middle row) Joseph Bertrand, Thomas Plunkett, George Harrington, Lorenzo Moore Jr., unidentified, Oliver Comtois Jr., Albert Tyler, Harry Emery, Thomas Barry, Ed Chase, William Frazer, and Oliver Comtois Sr.; (back row, in doorway) Joseph Flynn and unidentified.

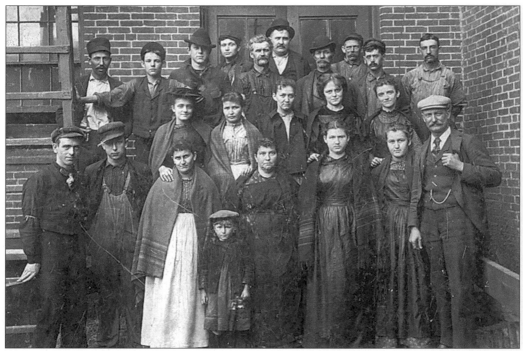

The only person identified in this *c.* 1900 photograph of Chapin Mill hands is overseer Big Jack White, front row at the far right. The workers are of various ages, but one rather hopes that the tyke in front is not one of them. The influx of workers to the Chapin Mill and the nearby Wood Mill, many of them French-speaking Canadians, necessitated the opening of the so-called Factory School in 1880 (see page 110).

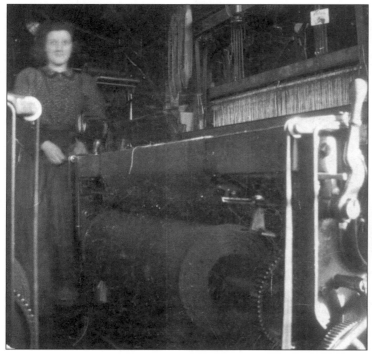

This young woman is most likely Alice Hinds LaPorte, who operated a loom at the Chapin Woolen Mill in the late 1890s. This ponderous loom was capable of producing carpets, blankets, and other heavy fabrics. She lived in the house pictured on page 50.

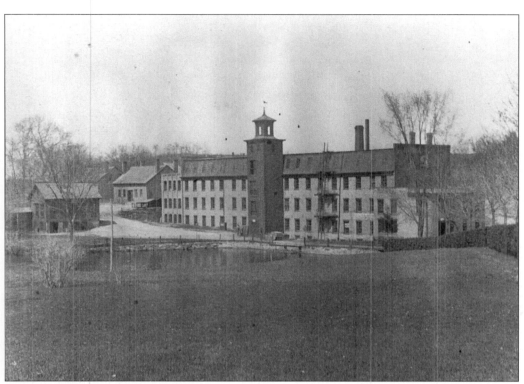

The Chapin Mill was powered by the Assabet River, the bed of which lay several hundred yards away. A sluice, still well-defined today, conveyed water into and through the mill at Hudson and Coburn Streets, which at various times produced cotton and woolen fabrics. In 1918, when it was the Whittaker Mill, fire partially destroyed it; the mill declined thereafter. Only part of the foundation exists today.

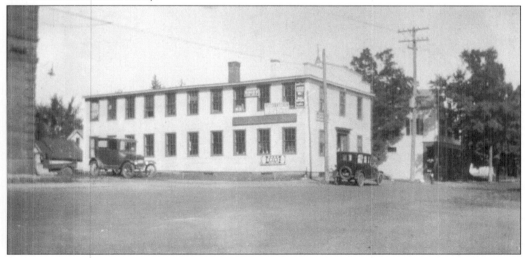

By the early 1920s, this building behind the town hall on Blake Street, where Josiah Proctor had made buttons, had been reduced from three and one-half floors to two floors. The signs suggest that it was in transition. The lowest sign bespeaks a "shoe shine parlor." Beginning in 1923, the building housed Frank St. Onge's plumbing shop. Since the 1950s, the basement has been Sawyer's Bowladrome.

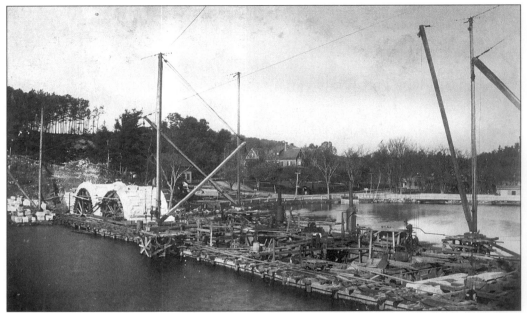

This and the following sequence of photographs depict the building of the Metropolitan Aqueduct, intended to convey water from the Wachusett Reservoir southeast through Northborough to another reservoir in Southborough. This late-1896 photograph shows a cofferdam stretching across the millpond formed by the Wood Mill dam on the Assabet River at Allen Street. David Wood's mansion stands out in the center of the picture.

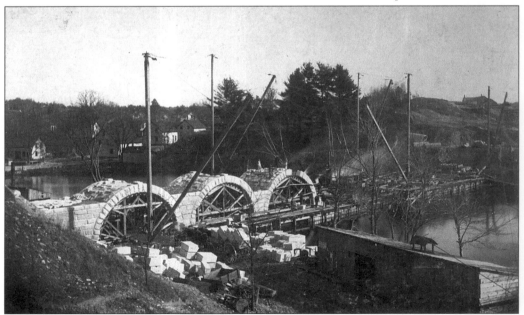

This view from the opposite bank shows the laying of the first three arches of the seven-arch structure that eventually carried water over the Assabet River. David Wood built and rented to his mill workers most of the houses that are visible. Much excavation remains to be done on the far side of the river, for the aqueduct was designed to run below ground level for several more miles.

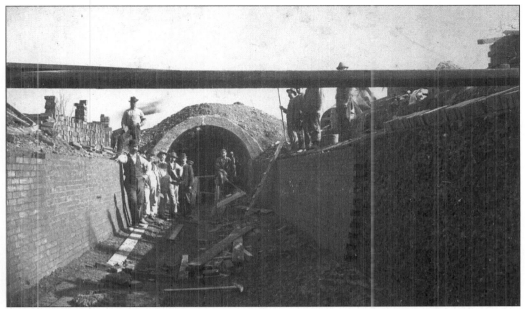

This photograph of the aqueduct shows the lining and the circular shape of the passage, as well as a number of workers, many of them evidently supervisory. During the two years required for the building of the seven-arch bridge, Northborough was the temporary home of a number of engineers. The pickax in the foreground is a reminder that most of the labor was of the back-breaking type.

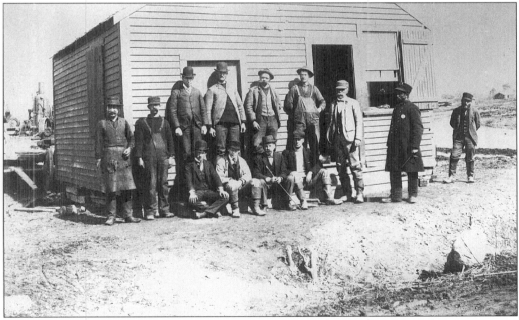

This picture suggests the cosmopolitan nature of an aqueduct work crew. Italian immigrants predominated among the 1,223 workers at the time of maximum employment. All of the men are wearing headgear, and presumably the derby hats and the relative finery of some constitute off-duty apparel.

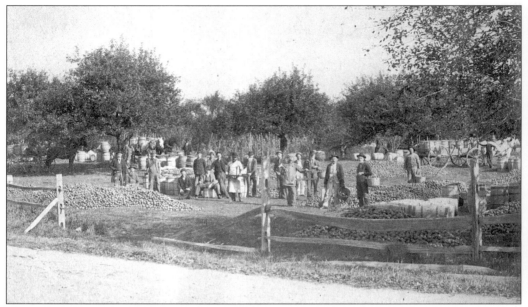

This image brings to mind the Robert Frost line "I am done with apple-picking now." When these laborers assembled for this 1880 photograph, their orchard occupied a corner of School and Summer Streets near the town center. In this highly organized endeavor of horses, wagons, barrels, and men, only the woman on the right is still at work. Today, Northborough's orchards are confined to Ball Hill beyond Route I-290 in the northwestern corner of town.

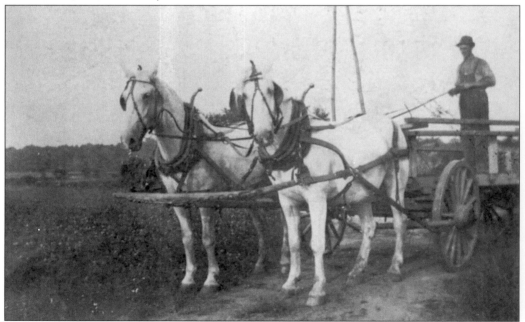

Hermon L. Sparrow leads his team on his Colburn Street farm c. 1907. Sparrow did significant retail business in "grain, feed, hay, and poultry supplies." He succeeded his father, Lewis Sparrow, and was in turn succeed by his son Hermon L. Sparrow Jr. on the farm. In the late 1960s, the younger Hermon Sparrow sold the farm to the developers of an industrial park adjacent to the new Route I-290.

It must have been fun for young Paul Brigham to accompany his grandparents George and Sarah Brigham on a milk run in the late 1920s. Members of this branch of the oldest Northborough family (see page 77) remain in town to this day.

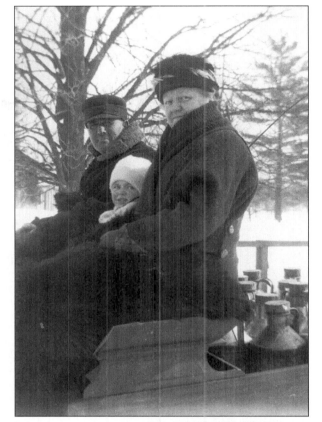

Henry Warren drove this butcher cart for A.E. Wallace in 1897, when this picture was taken. Warren later went into the laundry business. The activities of the Warrens from the end of the Civil War to the mid-1920s, as well as many other happenings in town, furnish subjects for his mother's diary (see page 92).

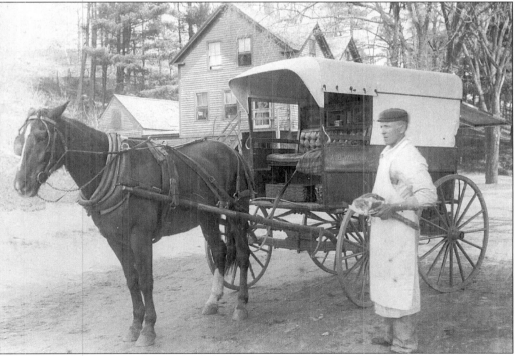

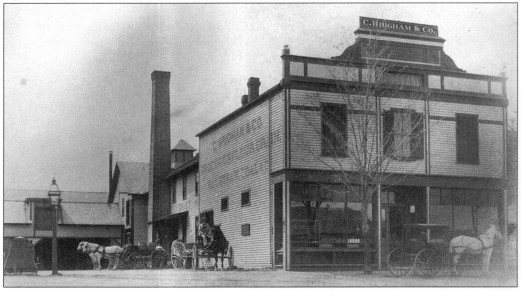

The opening of the town hall on the corner of Main and Blake Streets in 1868 encouraged the development of commerce nearby. In the early 1890s, Charles Brigham sold groceries, flour, grain, hay, straw, and coal—as indicated by the sign on the side of the building.

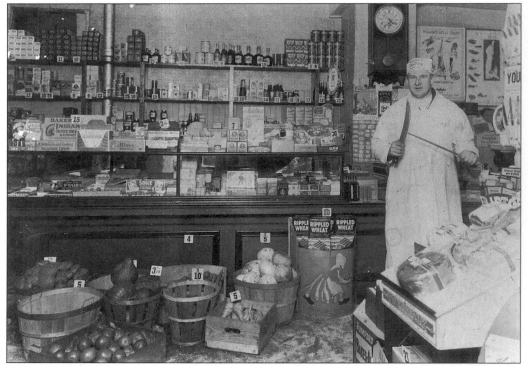

In 1898, the storefront of C. Brigham & Company became Peinze's Grocery Store. Many of the brand names seen in this photograph—Hires, Rumford, Baker, My-T-Fine—persist today, but the prices have increased considerably. The variety of produce and the advertisement for "a delicious and cooling summer drink" indicate that the time is late summer. Peinze's Grocery Store continued at this location for more than 60 years.

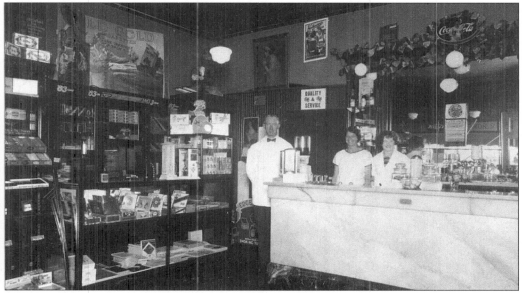

Thomas White poses inside his store in the Winn-Whitaker building with his clerks in the late 1920s. Margaret Walker and Ann Dyer Farrell, smiling from behind the marble counter, are prepared to dish out not only the old standbys—vanilla, chocolate, and strawberry—but also frozen pudding and maple-nut ice cream. White also appears as the drummer in the brass band picture on page 113 and in the Northborough Grange picture on page 127.

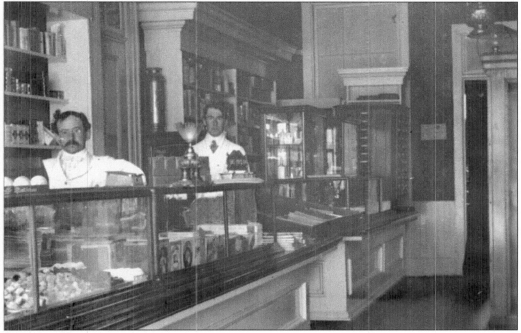

Claude T. Shattuck purchased the former E.W. Wood pharmacy in the town hall in 1898. This picture probably dates from the establishment's earliest years. It eventually turned into the archetypal American drugstore, with a soda fountain that attracted lively young customers. Shattuck's son Howard Shattuck succeeded him. Today, grandson Paul Shattuck continues to operate the pharmacy in a building across the street.

Monday Nov 28. 1921

Wm is 81 years old to day, and such a day I do not think I ever knew. It rained and sleeted all night and all day. our lovely trees are all broken up. the apricot the limbs are badly broken one cherry tree half of it lays on the ground. the mulberry is broken off at the ground, some of the apple trees are broken five maples are in awful shape the tops are so badly broken. every thing is loaded with ice, it is frozen on so that when the wind blows they snap and down they come last night was very windy and it has been to day. Alfred went to Worcester to work. he says we know nothing about the storm. Telephone wires are broken also telegraph and two of the Electric wires are broken and lay across our drive way. the wires are broken that go to the shop, so Henry says he dont know when they will be able to do any washing. not a car by to day. Olive carried Mrs Martins milk over, and Marion Rice came over to get some kerosine, as there are no electric lights to night, things will be worse in the morning as we hear the limbs on the trees break every little while.

Tues Nov 29

Stormed all day rain and sleet. our trees are all covered with ice and broken. Alfred staid at home the drive way is filled with branches broken from the trees. when the wood is worked up we shall have apple apricot Cherry Elm Hydrangea Maple Mulbery peach pear and walnut big Oak. Mr Alfred Wallace dild very suddenly this afternoon he was in town this morning. Olive went down to Mrs

Rosa Crosby Warren would probably be amazed at a reference to her "works," but her diary, composed over almost 60 years, deserves this designation. As she routinely detailed her daily life as a housewife and mother, the diary unselfconsciously reflects the changes in town life from the time of her marriage to William Warren in 1866 to shortly before her death in 1925. Her house on an embankment above West Main Street offered a handy perspective on the passing scene. Over the years, she went places on foot, by horse and wagon, by trolley, and eventually by automobile. She seldom failed to record the weather. This page describes the ravages of an ice storm in late November 1921.

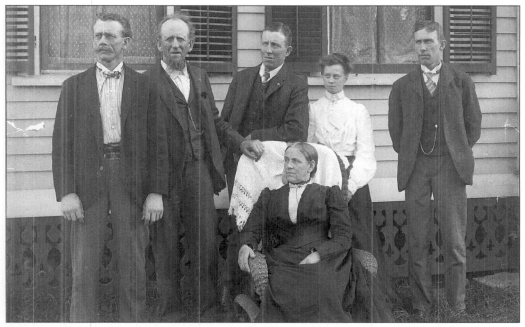

In the second decade of the 20th century, the Warren family pose outside their home at 173 West Main Street. Rosa Warren sits in front of the others, who are, from left to right, son Charles, husband William, son Henry, daughter Olive, and son Alfr0ed. An earlier picture of Henry Warren appears on page 89; William Warren also appears on the spraying rig on page 81 and on a parade float on page 120.

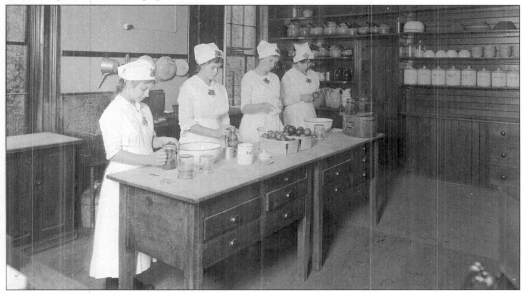

Four young women demonstrate their canning expertise in this 4H-sponsored activity of the World War I era. From left to right, they are Anna Carlson, Miriam Parmenter, Bessie Smith, and Caroline Lilley. Bessie Smith Murray also appears in the Grange photograph on page 127. In 1956, she gained the distinction of becoming the first Northborough woman elected to the Massachusetts General Court. In her term as state representative, she never missed a legislative session or a committee meeting.

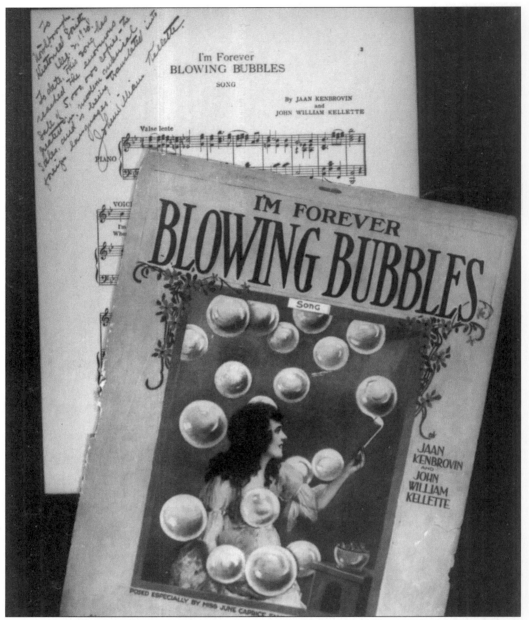

Born in Lowell in 1875 and orphaned at the age of nine, John William Kellette shined shoes and sold newspapers on the streets of Boston in his early teenage years. He first came to Northborough because an aunt lived here. He worked as a printer's devil, as a streetcar conductor, and in 1898 as a reporter for the *Worcester Telegram*. Enlisting in the army at the outbreak of the Spanish-American War, he sent back accounts of the action to the newspaper. For a year or two after the war, he operated a press out of his home. Leaving Northborough, he began to carve out a career by devising scenarios for silent Hollywood films and writing songs, the most popular of which, "I'm Forever Blowing Bubbles" (1919), made him a wealthy man. Kellette and his wife returned to town in 1918. In 1922, at the age of 47, he died at his home on 67 Main Street, having been permanently weakened by the yellow fever he contracted in the war. (Photograph courtesy of Francis Doyle Photography, Northborough.)

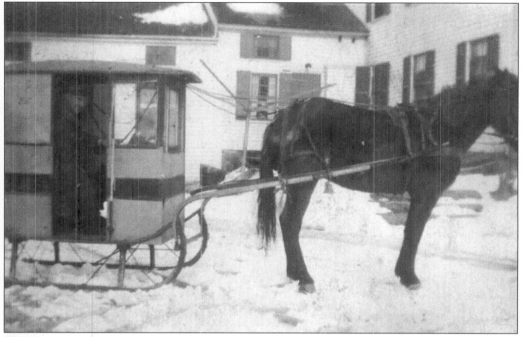

Shown are the two ways in which the Northborough post office delivered the mail in the 1920s. In this era, people did not so much battle the elements as adapt to them. Why clear snow from the roads when a sure-footed horse and a sleigh, above, stood ready for duty? In the summer, a c. 1920-vintage automobile, below, served the purpose. Although the population did not exceed 2,000 in this era, it was rather sparsely distributed within the town limits, and the route therefore wound through most of the town's 18.72 square miles.

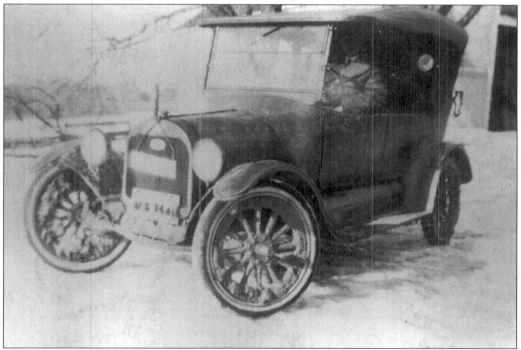

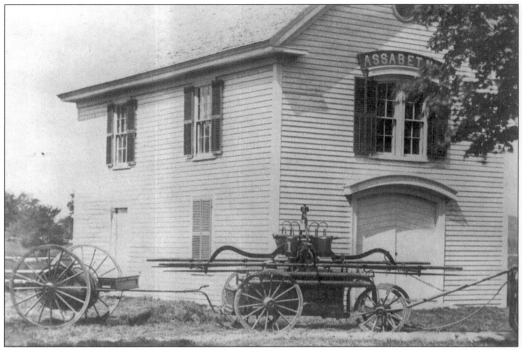

Engine No. 1 of the Assabet Engine Company, purchased in 1860, stands in front of the Hudson Street fire station. This building, which no longer exists, dates from 1884. For years after the station opened, the fire department maintained no horses, but rather appropriated them as necessary from nearby residents to pull engines to fires. The first motorized equipment was a Model T Ford truck acquired in 1918.

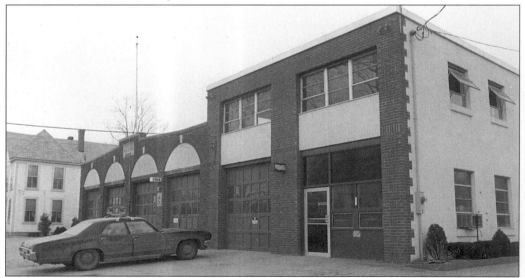

Beginning in 1926, Northborough's volunteer firefighters answered the call at this Church Street station, which replaced the one on Hudson Street. The right side of this building served as a station, albeit a narrow one, for the town's police department. By the time of the building's 50th anniversary, both departments had outgrown the facility, and each moved into more commodious quarters.

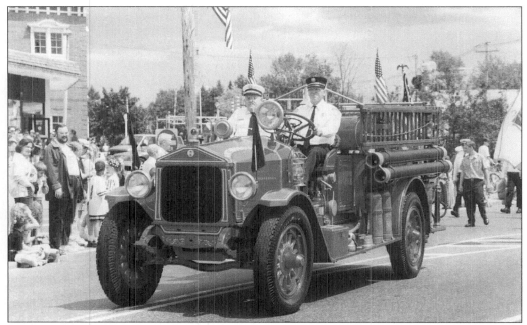

William Cluff and Paul Desautels maneuver a fully restored 1923 Maxim fire engine down Church Street during a recent Memorial Day parade. The pumper had served the fire department for 50 years when it was sold to the Northborough Firefighters' Association in 1973. It is now used for parades in many surrounding towns.

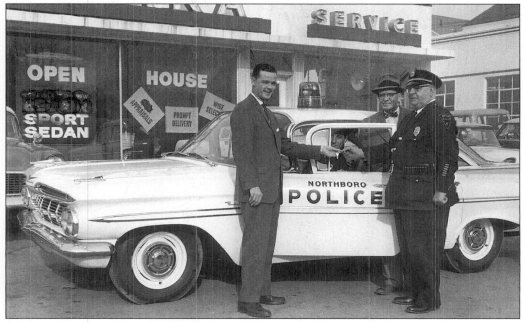

A dealer hands the keys of a new cruiser to Francis Bodreau, chief of police. In 1959, Bodreau commanded only two other full-time officers in the Northborough Police Department. Hector Giovannucci, half of his force, sits in the driver's seat. The other gentleman is Welcome Burbank, a selectman. By 1999, the force had grown to 20 uniformed officers, supplemented by an administrative secretary and seven dispatch personnel.

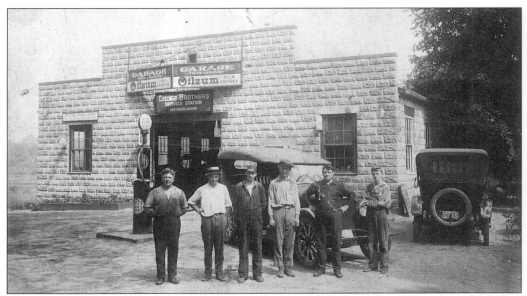

To service a Dodge or any other make *c.* 1916, automobile owners could call on these gentlemen. From left to right, they are Ernest Standish, Gus Carlson, unidentified, Kester Lindsay, Tom Lindsay, and unidentified. No longer under the aegis of the Dodge Brothers and no longer dispensing gasoline, this establishment continues the tradition of automotive repair as the WCD garage, named for the initials of three later owners.

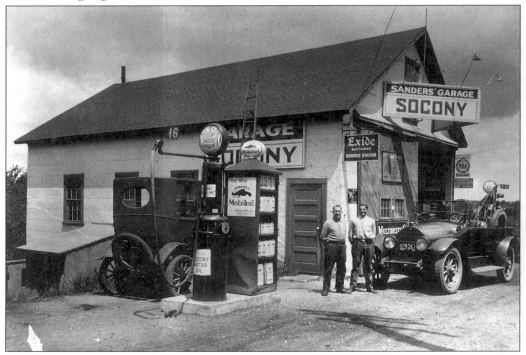

In this 1927 photograph, station owner Bob Sanders, left, and mechanic Ted Lawrence look proud of their establishment, its towing equipment, and its recognition by the National Automobile Association. More than 70 years later, under different ownership, the garage endures as a venerable and vine-covered structure on West Main Street.

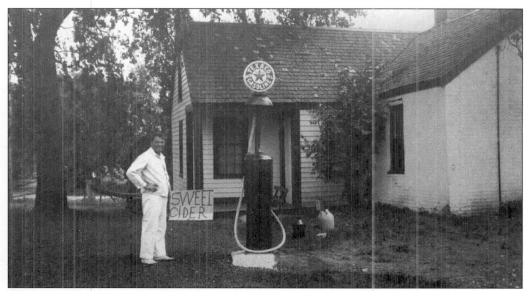

This picture was taken shortly after Fred and Eugenia Buck established their gasoline station at East Main and Bartlett Streets in 1919. While getting their tank filled, customers could also get their fill of cider from the Buck's mill. In 1931, when a new stretch of highway replaced East Main Street as part of the Boston Post Road, the Bucks had to relocate their station.

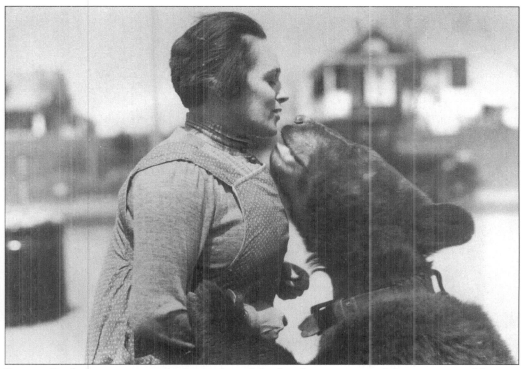

Eugenia Buck demonstrates which member of the family most enjoyed the company of the two bears that were added as an attraction in 1923. The town fathers, fearing for the safety of visitors to the station, forced the Bucks to part with the bears a year or two later.

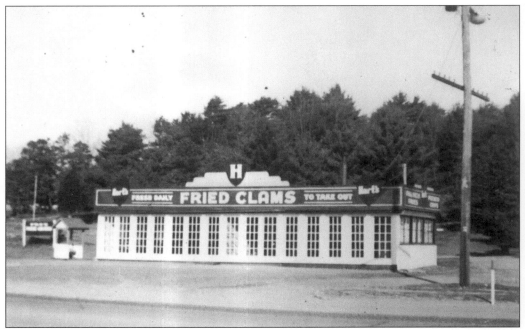

Hart's Fried Clams operated in the 1930s. This building, never an architectural gem, later deteriorated as a bar until it was swept from its site on West Main Street when Northborough tidied up its "Times Square" in the late 1960s.

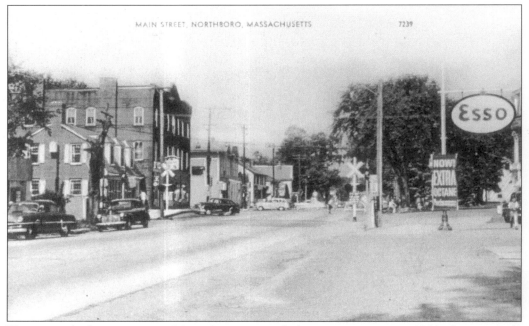

This view looking west on Main Street toward the town center in 1950 shows mostly commercial buildings. The structure on the left with the three dormers is the new home of the Northborough National Bank, which has not yet expanded into the three-story corner block. Trees planted in the 19th century still shade the facade of the town hall beyond the Esso station.

Five

CHURCH AND SCHOOL

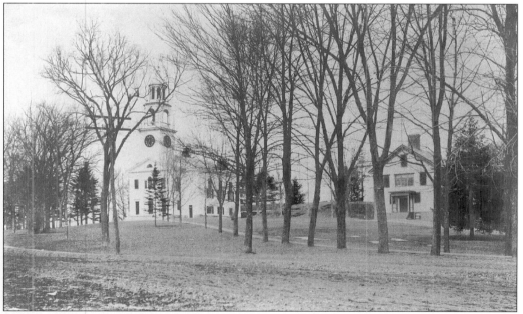

Religion and education are conjoined in this early-20th-century photograph. A tree-lined walk leads to the First Church, constructed in 1808 to replace the original meetinghouse near the same site. The building to the right served from 1870 to 1924 as the town's high school. The church building endured until a few days after Christmas of 1945, when a spectacular fire destroyed it. The present church is a replica.

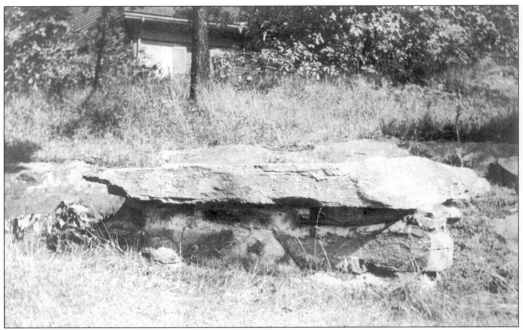

Behind the Unitarian Church and the partially visible Northborough High School is a stone platform bearing the inscription "Horse Block, 1746." Here, churchgoers could mount and dismount without disarranging their Sunday clothes. This picture dates from 1908, when the block no doubt was still in use. Today, the block remains near the drive behind the church.

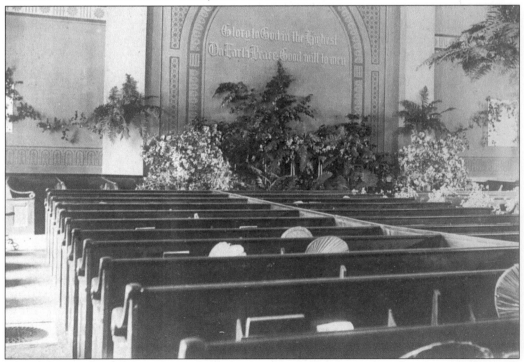

The elaborate floral decoration and the fans in the pews indicate that the photographer took this interior view of the 1808 First Church in the summer.

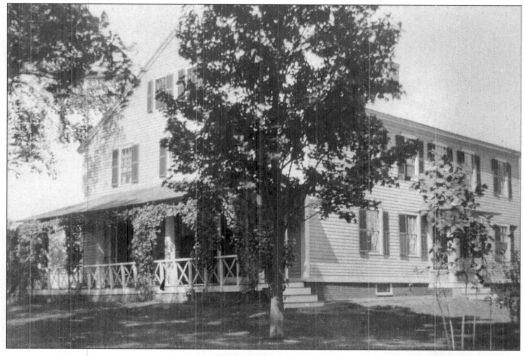

In the V formed by Pleasant and Church Streets stands this roomy house, the first home of Northborough's Evangelical Congregational church. In 1832, Dr. Joseph Allen of the First Church demonstrated an ecumenical spirit rare at the time by offering his church for this breakaway congregation's organizational meeting. The new building went up in a matter of weeks.

The second Evangelical Congregational church was erected in 1847 and was usually referred to as the "orthodox church" to distinguish it from the liberal Unitarian church, which continued to use the designation "congregational" also. Since its unification with Northborough's Baptists in 1948, it has been known as Trinity Church.

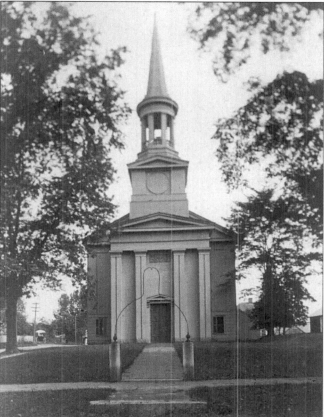

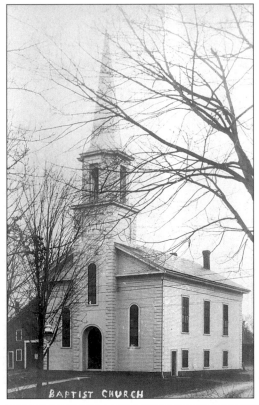

BAPTIST CHURCH

Beginning in 1860, several generations of Northborough's Baptists worshiped in this church at the corner of Main and School Streets. Its steeple crashed onto the front lawn during the September 1938 hurricane. Following the merger mentioned on the previous page, the Northborough Historical Society purchased the building and converted its upper level into a museum. The historical society has carefully preserved certain features, such as the 1874 George Stevens organ.

The first Roman Catholic Mass in Northborough was celebrated in June 1843 in the kitchen of Cornelius MacManniman's house at 92 Brigham Street, then only one story high. Few Catholics lived in Northborough until several years later, when Ireland's potato famine brought scores of Irish to town, the men working mostly as farm laborers, the women as domestic servants. Many of these immigrants lived in the Brigham Street area.

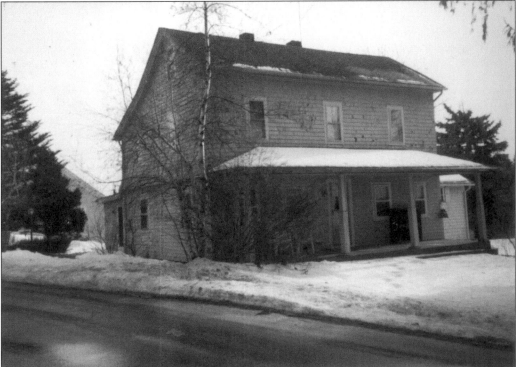

Northborough's Roman Catholics finally could boast of a proper church in 1883, when St. Rose of Lima's graceful steeple rose above Pierce Street—a steeple which, like that of the Baptist church, toppled in the 1938 hurricane. This church, with its damaged roof buttressed, continued in service until fears for the parishioners' safety and an expanding population necessitated a new St. Rose of Lima's Church on West Main Street. This building was demolished in 1968.

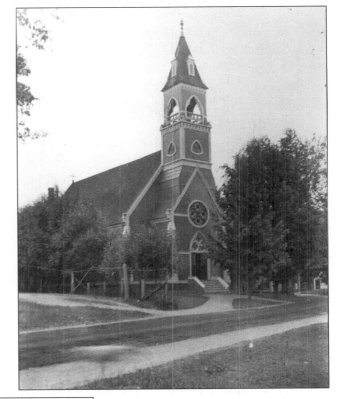

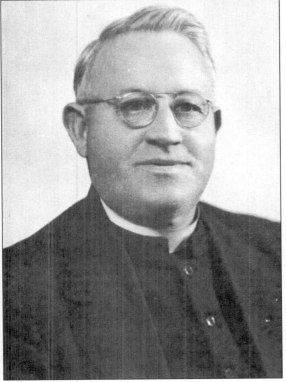

From 1935 to 1968, Rev. John J. Morrissey guided the destiny of the St. Rose of Lima Church. He was frequently referred to as "Northborough's Barry Fitzgerald," after the actor whose portrayal of a priest in the 1944 film *Going My Way* earned him an Academy Award. The sobriquet reflects his parishioners' appreciation of his kindness, wit, and Irish charm.

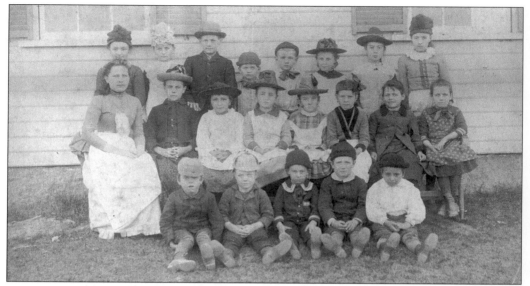

In the mid-1880s, the third East School stood at the intersection of Bartlett Street and Maple Street. Shown, from left to right, are the following: (front row) unidentified, Benjamin Haynes, Stephen Norcross, ? Richardson, and Herbert Mitchell; (middle row) Emma Hobart, Agnes Goodnow, Clara Mitchell, Emma Skelton, Marion Richardson, Edith Davis, Louise Goodnow, and Elsie Maccell; (back row) ? Skelton, Alice Bowes, Peter Goodnow, Charles Bowes, Benjamin Franklin Felt, Edith Bemis, Elsie Derosier, and Ada Skelton.

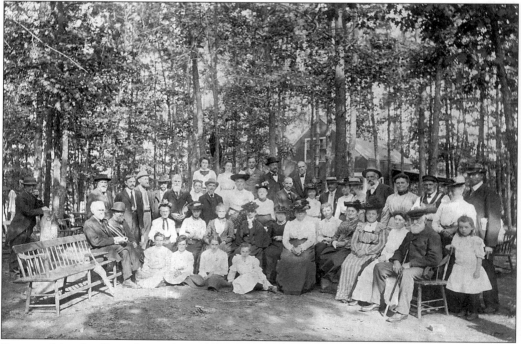

Because this school's graduates formed the East School Association, which functioned well into the 20th century, much is known about the school. The annual meetings usually took the form of summer picnics, complete with reminiscing, as was no doubt the case with this 23rd annual meeting of the organization on August 14, 1904.

The earliest Northborough schools were simple wooden buildings. This second-generation West School, erected in 1845 at the corner of Church and Brewer Streets, is one of two brick school buildings surviving today as private residences. A steep rise behind the school furnished excellent winter coasting for the students. The old chestnut tree on the opposite corner proved a handy landmark in a number of early town deeds.

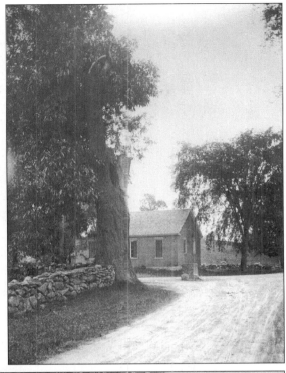

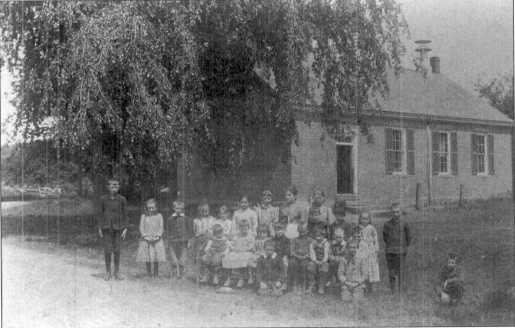

Several of the charges of Annie Potter, the West School teacher in the early 1890s, stand nearly as tall as she. Although we know that three of the pictured children are surnamed Allen (George Elmer, Mary, and Lucy), two are Baileys (Effie and Cora), and one is Wilford Valentine, they cannot be identified specifically. Annie Potter later served as principal of the new Hudson Street School.

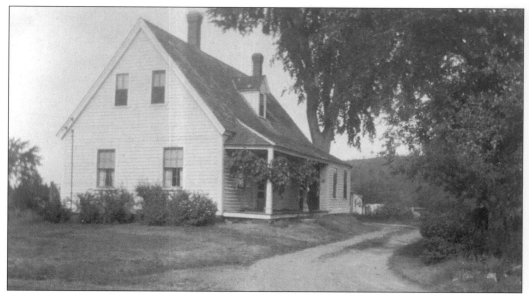

In the early 19th century, this frame building with its distinctive single dormer was the second of three North Schools. Judging from Gill Valentine's 1830 map of Northborough, it stood across Whitney Street from its brick replacement at the intersection of what is today Bearfoot Road. Moved a few hundred yards south to 192 Whitney Street, it continues in service as a private residence.

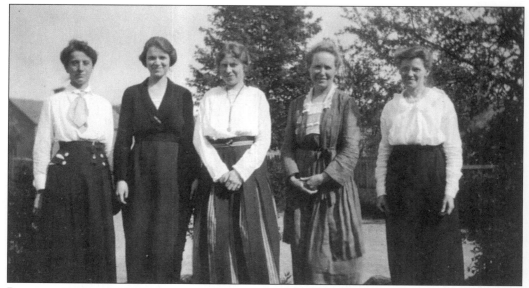

Between 1920 and 1922, these teachers constituted the staff at the Hudson Street School. They are, from left to right, Helen Corey, second grade; Mildred Gage, third and fourth grades; Mary Eldridge (also pictured on the cover), fifth and sixth grades; Marion Parmenter, special teacher; and Fanny Proctor, first grade. Fanny Proctor (pictured as a student on page 110) taught most of the town's children between 1890 and 1930—including her brother, Edwin Proctor (see page 63).

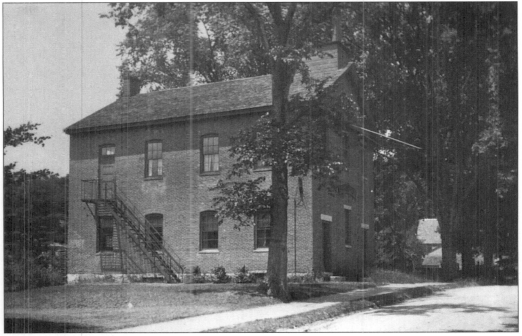

In 1838, Northborough opened its new brick District One school on School Street for the students who lived in the center of town. A bell in the cupola summoned them to classes. In 1895, when a new school opened on Hudson Street to serve most of the town's elementary school children, this building became the Grange Hall. It is shown here as the Grange Hall, without a rear addition that was later built.

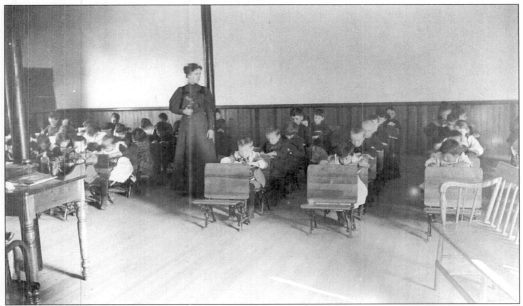

The teacher is Aurora A. Heath, who taught in the Hudson Street School after it opened in 1895, but this classroom is surely in the Factory School, where she labored earlier. The school subsequently acquired the more elegant designation of Woodside School, in reference to David F. Wood, whose nearby mill gave the name "Woodside" to the general surrounding area.

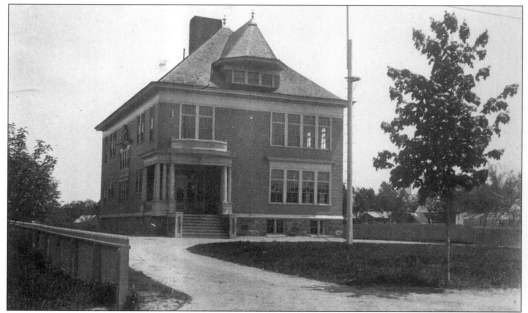

Although the Hudson Street School was fairly large, it contained only four classrooms. In its earlier years, adjacent grades were combined. As enrollment became larger, other expedients grew necessary. In the 1930s, a portable classroom on the grounds accommodated the overflow. Between 1895 and 1950, when the first modern elementary school opened, nearly all Northborough children attended this school. It was razed in 1983 in favor of a housing project for senior citizens.

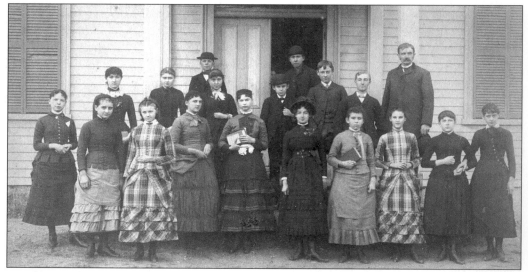

Northborough High School students pose with their teacher Albert Gray, middle row at the far left, on December 1, 1884. The students are, from left to right, as follows: (front row) Jennie Morse, unidentified, Fanny Proctor, Evelyn Potter, Lucy MacMurtrie, Jennie Chapin, Belle Duplisse, Emma Proctor, Annie Potter, and Alice Rathbun; (middle row) Eva Hastings, unidentified, unidentified, Charles Valentine, Charles White, and Will Eager; (back row) unidentified and Philip Hilliard. At this time, Philip Hilliard and Jennie Morse were already sweethearts (see page 48). For Hilliard's activity later as a selectman, see page 14.

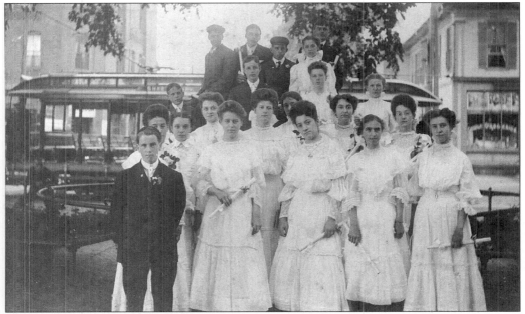

With an open-air trolley car behind them, the 1905 grammar school graduates face the town hall. Pictured, from left to right, are the following: (first row) Edward Gallagher, Cora Collins, Cora Chabot, Hazel Faulkner, and Effie Adams; (second row) Elva Warren, Flora Dumont, Eila Kelly, Sally Hatch, Mary Gallagher, Hazel Neilly, and Daun Neilly; (third row) Alpheus Adams, Albert Mentzer, Ruth Harrington, and Isabel Thompson; (fourth row) Ralph DeArmond, Everett Mentzer, unidentified, Elsie Brown, and Irving Balcom.

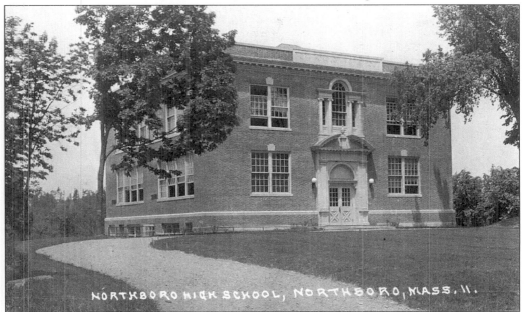

In 1924, the high school on the First Church Common gave way to this new brick school on Main Street, which in March 1938 was gutted by fire. The following year, a larger brick Northborough High School rose on the same site. In 1959, the latter building reverted to use as a junior high school; today, it serves as the town office building.

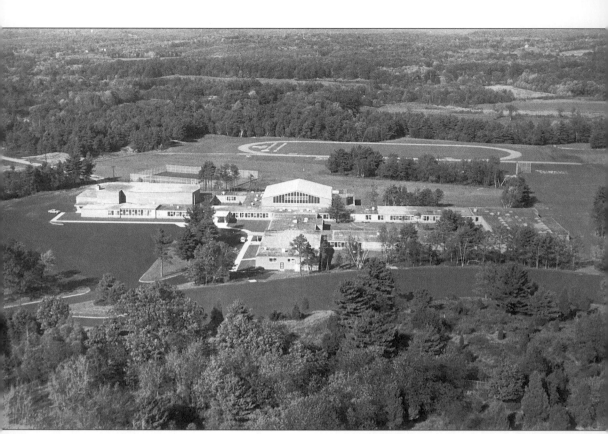

Northborough High School ceased to exist in 1959, when classes commenced in the new Algonquin Regional High School on Bartlett Street, seen in the fall of that year in this aerial view. Northborough had joined with Southborough and Berlin to form a regional school district in 1954, although Berlin withdrew a year later. The faculty for the new school was gathered from the former Northborough High School and Peters High School in Southborough, with some new additions. The 444 students of Algonquin Regional High School found a new breadth of programs in science, the performing arts, and interscholastic athletics. Some 40 years later, after the addition of a wing and an increase to nearly 600 students, plans were evolving to replace the now inadequate building.

Six

CELEBRATION AND
RECREATION

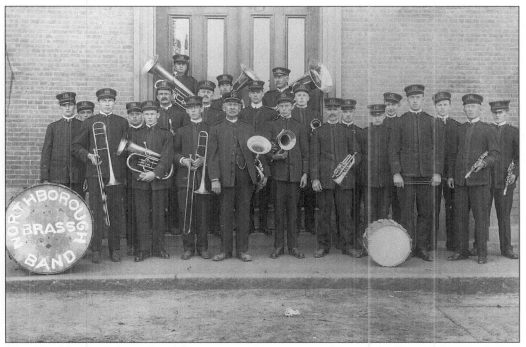

The Northborough brass band lines up in this c. 1911 photograph. From left to right are Ernest Moore, George Chapdelaine, Elmer Bemis, Charles Brigham, Loring Harrington, Charles Murray, Solomon Goddard, Stephen Norcross, E. Montford Brigham, Lindsay Jones, Louis Wheeler, Norman Potter, ? Wheeler, Laurian Lowe, Sidney Walls, Fred Garfield, Clarence Wood, Walter Peinze, Carl Peinze, Tom White, Martin Ryan, Walter Brigham, and Waldo Bemis.

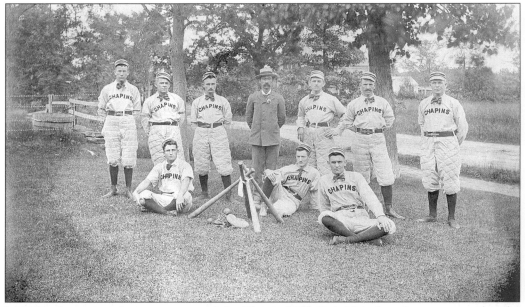

In 1893, these nine players represented the Chapin Mill. Only Napoleon Jacques, seated in the center, has been identified. The equipment is interesting. The players wear neckerchiefs. Could their seemingly quilted trousers be advertisements for the mill's products? The team's catcher enjoys the benefits of what was then a recent innovation: a protective mask. He also uses a mitt, but no gloves for the rest of the team are in evidence.

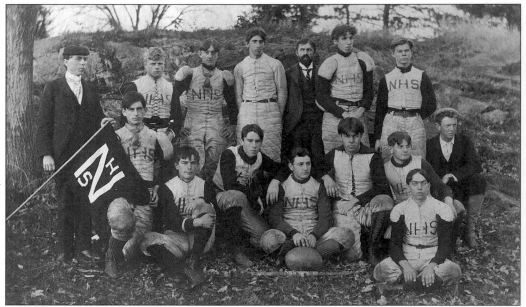

Standing with the Northborough High School football team of 1901 is George F. Blood, school principal, back row, third from right. Team members, from left to right, are as follows: (front row) George Corey; (middle row) Frank Norton, Joseph Gallagher, Joseph Murray, Bernard Burdette, Addison Moore, Harry Allen, George LaPorte, and Frank Eames; (back row) George Proctor, Arthur Corey, Homer Prouty, George Snow, and Elmer Allen. Missing from this picture are Guy Trundy, George Simpson, and George Haskell.

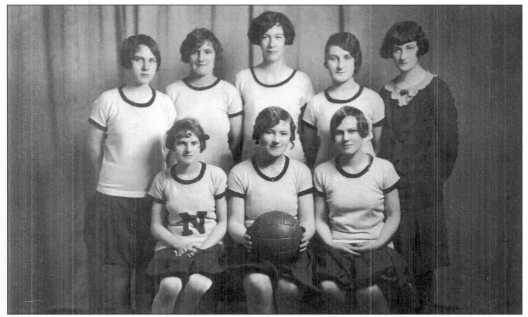

The Northborough High School girls' basketball team of 1928–1929 includes, from left to right, the following: (front row) Gertrude Brady, Isabel Ford, and Esther Clark; (back row) Winifred Clark, Alice Smith, Marion Buckley, Priscilla LaPorte, and Estelle Garrity. Unfortunately, information about the team's level of success is lacking.

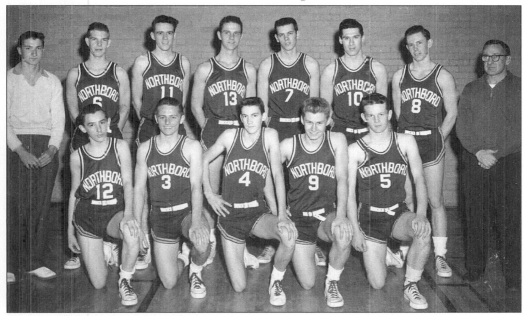

Northborough High School boys' basketball teams enjoyed phenomenal success in the mid-1950s. Shown is the 1955–1956 team, which went unbeaten in 30 regular season games. Shown, from left to right, are the following: (front row) Robert Keigwin, Robert Stebbins, William George, Francis Aldonis, and Jonathan Field; (back row) manager P. Klein, Burton Gustafson, Robert Fouracre, Donald Blakely, Junie George, William Gagnon, David Gauvin, and coach John Clark.

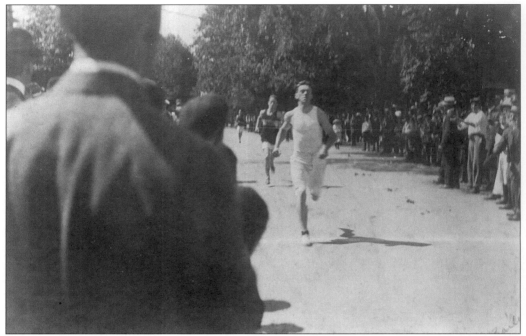

The runner crossing the finish line in the July 4, 1909 holiday race is Everett Mentzer, at age 20. Mentzer, who grew up on one of the town's larger farms (see page 35), later owned several horses, some of which can be seen on page 119. His interest in growing things led him to a career as a florist. He is part of the grammar school class from a few years earlier on page 111.

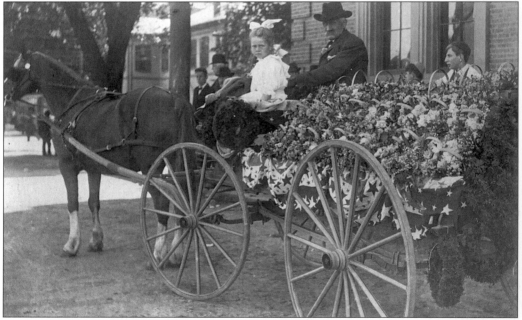

John J. Wood was a teamster in days when the term literally meant driving a team. Here, he needs only one horse to deliver Memorial Day flowers, c. 1908. As young children have a way of doing, Louise Eldridge has decided that her grandfather will be better off with her assistance on this mission. She also appears in the cover photograph.

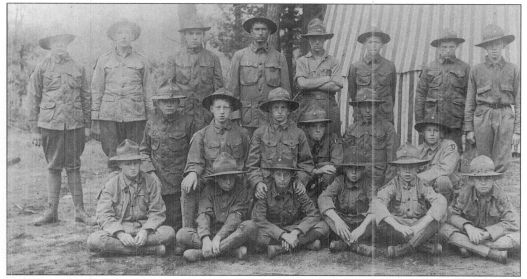

Northborough Boy Scouts pose in front of their tent in this c. 1920 photograph. From left to right, they are as follows: (first row) Norman Smith, Jim Duffy, Gordon Crossley, Hillard Poland, Chester Warren, and Carl Carlson; (second row) Vernon Maccabee, Adelbert Cox, Vernon Bigelow, unidentified, Howard Shattuck, and Allen Johnson; (third row) Russell Tilley, Albert Nelson, Kenneth Maccabee, Carl Eldridge Sr., Carroll Blakely, Robert Proctor, Clifford Sprott, and Harold Sargent.

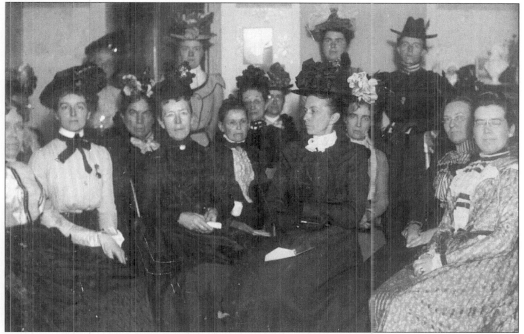

These members of the Northborough Woman's Club, c. 1903, make up fewer than one-third of the total strength of 50 at that time. Some of these women had been charter members in 1894. Their earnestness and erect carriage are as striking as the extravagance of some of their hats. Although its style has changed considerably, the present-day Northborough Woman's Club continues to function as vigorously as ever.

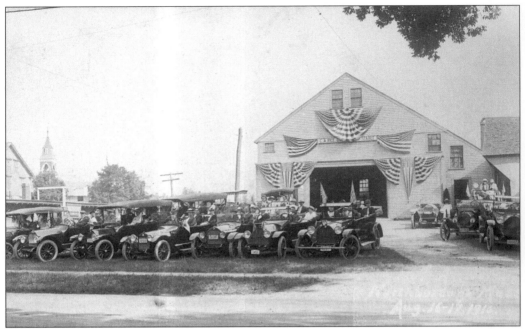

Dozens of people in parked automobiles await Northborough's 150th anniversary parade. In 1916, the automobile was beginning to challenge the horse and wagon. No horse is in sight in front of the C.A. Rice Livery Stable on Main Street. A decade later, this building was redesignated as the Walker Brothers Garage. Today, an Exxon station occupies the site.

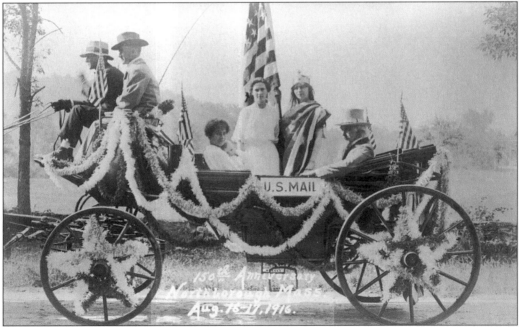

This float in the August 16, 1916 parade represents the U.S. mail. Mounted on the float, from left to right, are driver Dr. E.W. Bradley of Marlborough, Dorrace Lever, Dorothy Lever, a very young Marjorie Lever, Elizabeth Ryan, assistant postmaster Mary Ryan, and postmaster Martin H. Ryan.

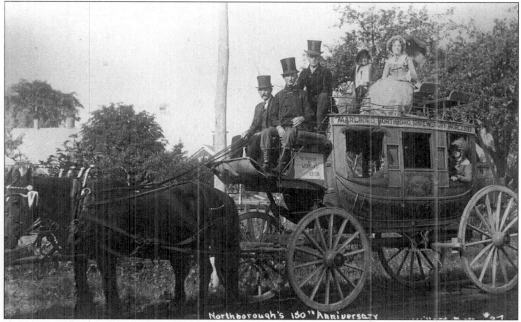

The Northborough Woman's Club entry in the parade is a stagecoach driven by Henry Blakely. It is drawn by four of Everett Mentzer's horses. Assisting the driver are Fred French and Charles Bigelow. Six club members occupied the coach, which had been used on runs between Marlborough and Worcester many years earlier. The prominent woman on the top is believed to be Mrs. Thornton Mentzer.

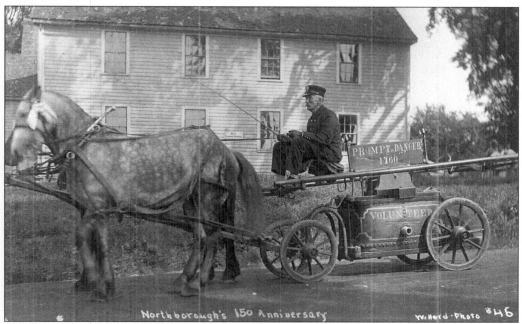

At age 82, George B. Wood was the oldest person in the parade. He is driving the oldest piece of Northborough firefighting equipment, at the time 76 years old, while passing in front of the Capt. Samuel Wood house, at age 167 one of the oldest and most notable houses in town.

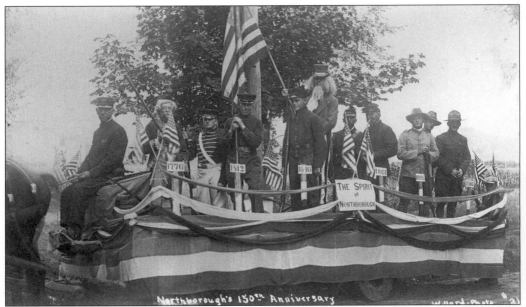

"The Spirit of Northborough" depicts the town's representation in the nation's wars. Participating were (not in order) William Warren, Harry Allen, George Proctor, Edwin Proctor, Chester Smith, Eben Paul, Winfred Stone, Tarble Haskell, Allyn D. Phelps, Henry Warren, George Walls, Lloyd Brigham, and Fred Proctor. Frederick Van Ornum, the school superintendent, portrays Uncle Sam. There are more names than there are faces in the photograph: did one or two supernumeraries have to stay behind?

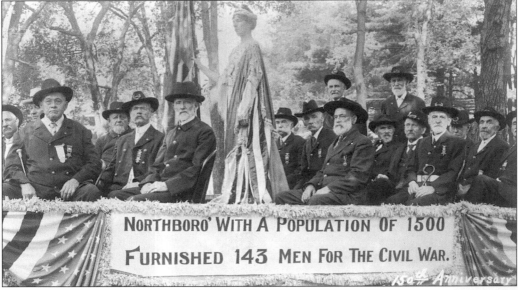

This float celebrates the impressive number of townsmen who served in the Civil War. The veterans representing the Joe Johnson Post No. 96 of the Grand Army of the Republic are (not in order) George Allen, John Johnson, Henry Burdett, Hazon Leighton, William Bemis, Cyrus Mentzer, Orin Bailey, Daniel Sawyer, Asa Fay, Walter Valentine, Peter Gamache, William Warren, John Hart, Levi Whitcomb, and Guilford Heath. Annie Heath portrays the "Goddess of Liberty."

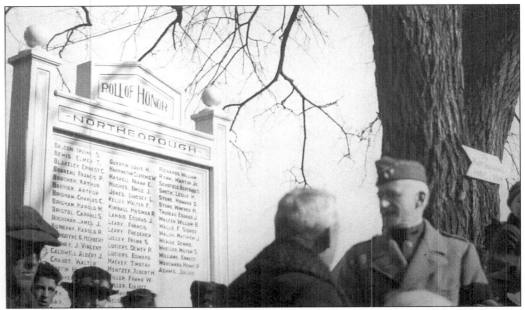

It is January 27, 1919, and Reverend Kent of the Unitarian church is greeting Gen. Clarence E. Edwards, commander of the 26th Yankee Division, at an impromptu reception. The reception was arranged quickly when it was learned that Edwards would pass through town. Several of the World War I veterans whose names appear on the roll of honor in the background served under Edwards.

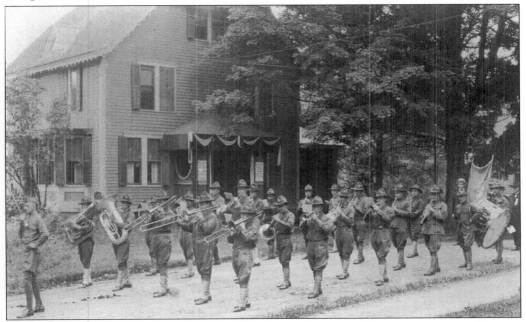

The official celebration in honor of Northborough's returning veterans took place on Tuesday, June 17, 1919. In the morning, a parade that was led by this band formed on Church Street and proceeded to Assabet Park, where young women of the town pinned bronze medals on each of the returned soldiers. A dinner, a reception, a concert, and a military ball ended the day's festivities.

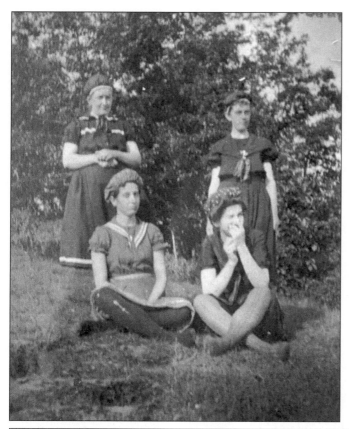

What are these young women sternly contemplating? It seems that they have come together on the bank of Bartlett Pond to consider whether or not to take a dip. Or will it, considering their bathing costumes, be more of a modest wade?

This couple is enjoying a canoe ride on a pond (presumably Bartlett Pond) on a summer day early in the 20th century. Bartlett Pond was formed by the damming of Stirrup Brook, which flows south from Little Chauncey Pond, at Bartlett Street. Often alleged to be the creation of Daniel Wesson, who probably had the existing spillway constructed in the 1880s, Bartlett Pond appears on an 1870 map (see page 2).

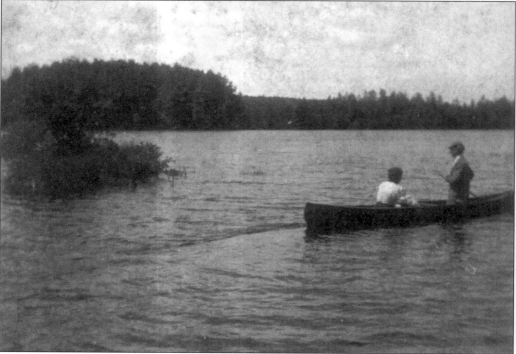

On July 18, 1891 a young lad has found an ideal place of contemplation on the bank of Solomon Pond (named for a Native American who, according to Northborough's first historian, Peter Whitney, drowned in it). Let us give the boy the benefit of the doubt and assume that he *has* invited the girl to sit beside him, but that she, fearful of damage to dress or bow, has refused.

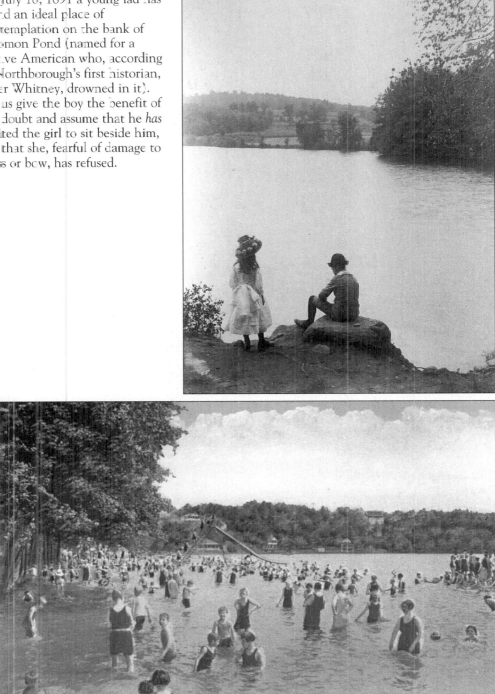

In the years c. 1930, when people no longer had to be rich or eccentric to own an automobile, places such as Solomon Pond became teeming recreational centers, as this postcard indicates. Today, public access to what this postcard euphemistically calls the "beach," is restricted, and bathers tend to repair to Big Chauncey Pond in neighboring Westborough.

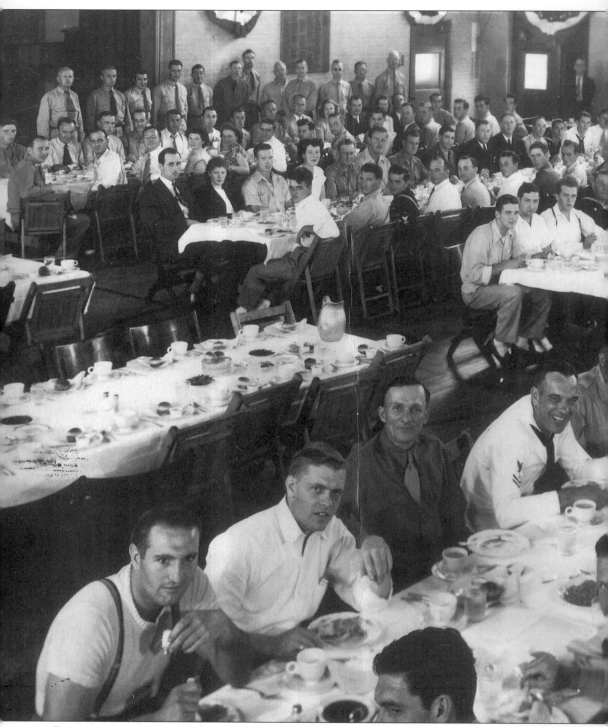

Because many veterans did not return home until months after the end of World War II, the committee in charge of honoring them decided to celebrate their return on July 4, 1946. In the morning, Wheeler's Band and the Lyman School Band from neighboring Westborough led a parade through town. This photograph shows the gymnasium of Northborough High School

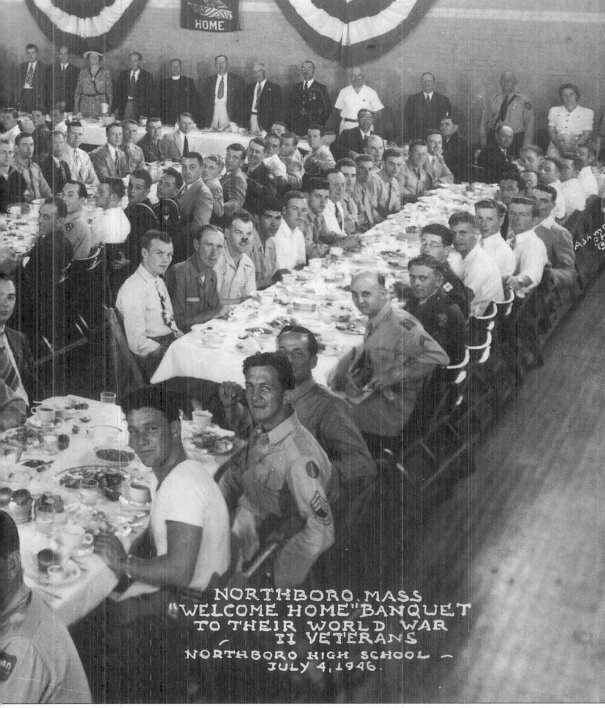

NORTHBORO, MASS
"WELCOME HOME" BANQUET
TO THEIR WORLD WAR
II VETERANS
NORTHBORO HIGH SCHOOL —
JULY 4, 1946.

around noon, as the veterans proceed to devour a turkey dinner. Although the diners are mostly men, a few women are present to attest to their military service. Sporting events and an evening dance rounded out this memorable day.

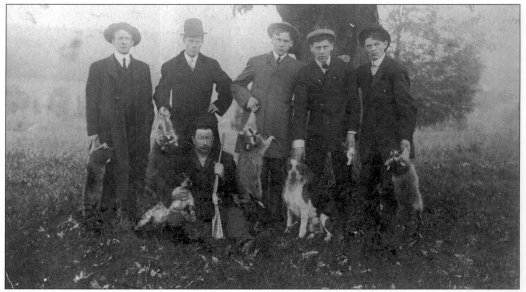

These lads have bagged at least four raccoons. Raccoons were sought for their flesh and their pelts, but their fondness for corn and melons also made them the farmers' enemy. Perhaps these young men hunted mainly for sport. More than a century later, it is difficult to know their motive.

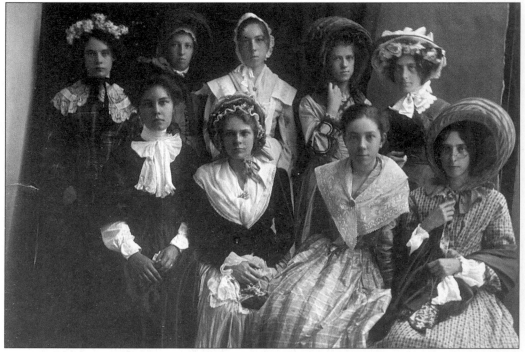

The cast of this early-20th-century dramatization of *Cranford*, Elizabeth Gaskell's novel of mid-19th century English village society, has assembled for a formal portrait. The players, from left to right, are as follows: (front row) Mary Allen, Marie Barnes, Elizabeth Richardson, and Annie Haskell; (back row) Josephine Talbot, Louisa Coffin, Ellen Richardson, Evelyn Proctor, and Hattie Haskell.

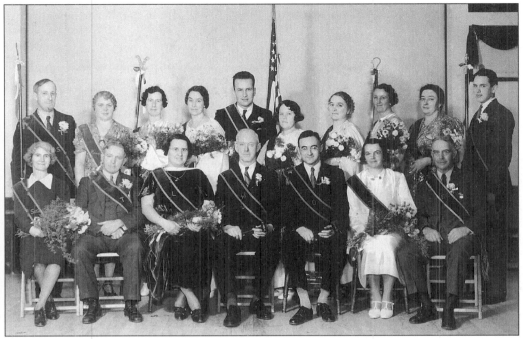

The officers of the Northborough Grange display their fine array in this 1938 photograph. From left to right, they are as follows: (front row) Florence Bemis, Willis Wheeler, Bessie Murray, Thomas White, Robert Brigham, Marjorie Buckley, and Clarence Buckley; (back row) Fred Leary, Mabel Brigham, Blanche Govin Walsh, Cora O'Brien, Harold Mayberry, Ruth Elphick, Eva White, Kathryn McClintock, Maude Mason, and Elmer Valentine Jr.

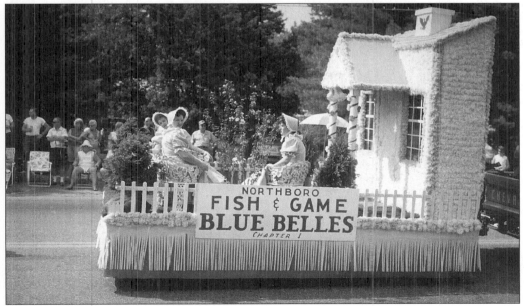

Northborough's most spectacular parade commemorated the town's bicentennial in 1966. This float is one of nearly 50 that dazzled spectators the afternoon of Sunday, August 21, 1966. In the opinion of many, community spirit crested at an all-time high during the preparations for and the carrying out of this celebration.

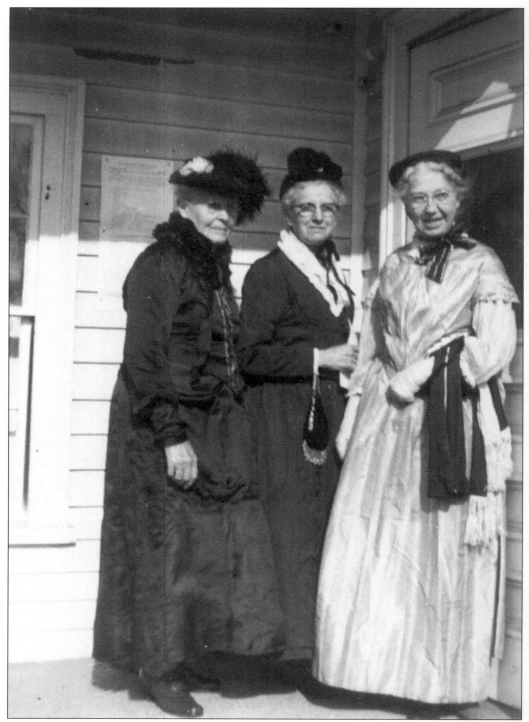

Outfitted for the town's bicentennial are three of Northborough's grand ladies. From left to right, they are Marion Parmenter, Helen Corey (seen much earlier in her life on page 108), and Margaret Sherman. All had been teachers, all were benefactors of the Northborough Historical Society, and all made significant contributions to the history of Northborough.